BROKEN *for* BATTLE

EMBRACE GOD'S BEST
TO LIVE A VICTORIOUS LIFE

KESHIA KIRKSEY

All Scriptures are taken from the KJV unless otherwise noted.

ISBN 13: 979-8-5600105-3-9

Printed in the United States of America

Contact Info:
Keshia Kirksey
P.O. Box 214214
Auburn Hills, MI 48321-4214
(734) 215-5564
www.KeshiaKirksey.com

DEDICATION

This book is dedicated to the two most influential people in my life: my wise and humorous father, Jerry W. Hendon, and my beautiful, delicate, and loving mother, Annie L. Hendon. These two incredible people created me from a pure, God-fearing, deep, intimate place, and from their hearts and spirit, I was conceived. For this, I'm grateful, and I thank you both.

Although you both possess diverse qualities, I have them all inside of me, and they have worked as weapons both for and against me throughout my journey. Not knowing the power you possess and not understanding how to use what you have can many times work against you instead of for you.

Romans 8:18 says, "For I reckon that the sufferings of this present time are not worthy to be compared with the glory which shall be revealed in us." My mom gave me this Scripture years ago and said, "Keshia, get this Scripture in your spirit. It's going to bless you one day."

My mom was intentional about pouring God's Word and love into her children. I learned at an early age that God was real and powerful and so was the devil, but God is always greater. I was taught that God manifested Himself in the flesh and sent His Son Jesus on earth to set an example, and He gave His life so that my sins could be forgiven. I was taught that without faith, it is impossible to please God. I was taught that God put something inside of me that the world needs. I was taught that being used by God was the greatest privilege on this earth, and I was taught in all things to give thanks.

My mom also taught me that no matter what you have, you won't enjoy it unless you share it. And most of all, I was taught love is powerful when you experience God's love.

With my mom pouring all these powerful nuggets into me, I broke Romans 8:18 down into what I thought it meant, and this is how I perceived it: no matter how bad things are right now, and no matter how low I get and how dark and hopeless I feel, if I can just endure through the hard times, I will see something so much greater than what I've seen, done, and experienced.

As an adult, it gave me a sense of hope because to think that God could get anything good out of the ugly, nasty, and terrible things I've been through was unbelievable. But it's in His Word, and since my mom believed it, so did I. This Scripture has blessed me throughout my life because no matter how low I've been, there was always something deep down inside of me that knew if I could just survive these hard seasons and storms, God could use these things to get the glory from what the devil designed to destroy me.

I always wanted to be used by God in a special way, but I never thought it was possible for me after all the negative things that my life had produced. There is a great price to be paid for God's glory and anointing. I wanted it so badly, but I was always too afraid to accept it for myself.

CONTENTS

MY DELICATE FLOWER

You kept a lovely garden
A garden of the heart
You planted all the good things
That gave me my first start
You turned me to the sunshine
And encouraged me to dream
Fostering and nurturing seeds of self-esteem
Your constant good examples taught me right from wrong
Markers for my pathway
To last my whole life long
Once the storms and the rain came, I had to stand up and be
tough
One by one your delicate petals told the winds they were to
rough
The reflections of your past reveal how you were made
Our memories will remain forever; I promise they will never
fade.

In loving memory of my beautiful mother, my delicate
flower,

Annie Lucille Ledwell Hendon

INTRODUCTION

Fine glass is a delicate beauty. Some people find rare crystals and fine glass on their ventures of travel around the world. They bring it back to their places of comfort and store it on display so they can look at it, admire it, and talk about it.

This beautiful work of art brings a sense of accomplishment to the one who has obtained it. It is not often used day to day for fear of breaking it. It's reserved for special occasions.

Once the fine glass is broken, there is no further use for it. The once beautiful and delicate glass is tossed or disposed of, and the user is now left to search for another that is equally or more beautiful than the last. If the user keeps the broken glass, it not only seems to be a waste of space but also serves as a constant reminder that he or she was careless and responsible for the damage of such a precious beauty.

I represent these broken pieces. Besides, my mom's been telling me for as long as I can remember, "Keshia, you're a diamond." When my mom first started saying I was a diamond, I wasn't sure what she meant because I was so young. She was so excited to tell me I was a diamond. Each time, she said it like it was the first time she ever had. It made me feel special to hear her say it. Diamonds are both expensive in value and appealing to the eye, so I welcomed the thought of such great characteristics.

By the time I reached teenage years, I hated to hear my mom say I was a diamond because the process of becoming a diamond was so painful, but she saw my worth while I was still in my process. So, she continued to say it.

The process to become a diamond is not quick. It takes time because it must be tested and proved through the fire, storms, and rain of life. Being a diamond meant enduring the dark places. Being a diamond meant developing and learning in the dark. Being a diamond meant to take a lickin' and keep on tickin'.

My mom saw the beauty of my diamond before I did. I'm not sure if my mom said I was a diamond because of actual events and situations or if she observed all the areas along the way that I stood out in a rare way. It didn't matter to me why she said it or how she knew because I believed everything she said to me, so I simply believed her and was just accustomed to hearing her say it.

What I didn't know along my journey was that all those broken pieces were not fine glass but rare diamonds. Diamonds are made by enduring extreme heat and pressure. Diamonds are known to cut glass, but glass will not cut any diamond. No matter how many pieces you break a diamond into, its value remains.

I was once delicate like the fine glass, but after years of molestation, sexual abuse, loss, and depression, I'm convinced that I am a diamond. Not only am I a diamond but I'm also broken and shattered into many pieces, and each broken piece of my diamond was designed to work as a weapon against the kingdom of darkness.

This serves as my life story.

CHAPTER 1
Foundations Are Important

My dad and mom were high school sweethearts and were excited to begin their journey together as husband and wife. They were young, inexperienced, and broke, but I was their first-born blessing. My dad was from Louisiana and came to Michigan as a teenager to begin a life of his own. My dad's birth father, Link Hendon, died when my dad was young, so he didn't get the opportunity to know him growing up. Leaving his wife, Rosie, to raise my father and his three siblings alone. Rosie was a God-fearing, sanctified, Holy Ghost-talking, prophesying woman of God, and she was serious about her business.

I believe that it's important for children to grow up with their father. Although single women have gracefully held down the position, it is my opinion that a woman can't teach a boy how to be a man. Just like it's a woman's job to teach a girl how to be a woman. Having a father in the home gives a visible example of how to be a leader and how to submit to leadership, how to be responsible, and how to treat a lady. These things can certainly be learned in a single-parent home, but having your father present gives a unique insight regarding family structure and balance.

My dad was in his early teens when he moved to Michigan. When he arrived, he met Pastor Robert L. Williams, the senior pastor of Deliverance Mission Apostolic Faith Church, and his sweet wife, Edith.

They took him in as their own, and my dad began his life of ministry in the apostolic doctrine. My dad is a wise man, a peacemaker, a giver, and has a high sense of discernment. Whether you were a kid or an adult, he was able to see areas that kept people divided or in bondage and would find a way to bring joy to any situation. My childhood was full of examples of him demonstrating these characteristics in our family.

I remember a time when my dad saw all of the neighborhood kids outside playing with the newest fashion and fads. Because he was the sole provider, we only had the bare necessities. We rarely could afford to have anything new. So, my dad came up with the brilliant idea to make his kids feel like we finally had something we could be proud of. He went to the Salvation Army and found a random mixed match pair of roller skates for each of us. He cut the toes out of each pair because they were not any of our sizes and used my mom's zigzag scissors so all the toes looked like shark teeth. He used all sorts of colored magic markers and transformed each one of the skates into a shark, a dinosaur, an alligator, and a lion.

My dad knew he had to set the stage and prepare us for our roller-skate extravaganza before we went outside and showed them off to all the kids on the block.

He gathered us all together and told us he had a surprise for us, and we started screaming with excitement. He said, "What I have for you is so special that all the kids on the block are going to be jealous because they never had anything like it before." My dad's prep talk took so long that we were getting impatient. He even offered a question and answer session. He couldn't afford for this to go wrong, so he spent lots of time pouring encouragement into us before sending us outside to try it out. We couldn't imagine what this surprise could be. What we did know is that whatever it was that it was special, and everybody would want one. The power of what you tell a child will shape their future. As adults, we shape their conscious mind as well as their subconscious mind. We believed anything our dad said. So, he gave us the skates, and we were so excited that we put those skates on and went outside.

The neighborhood kids laughed at us nonstop. I can still hear them teasing us and calling us names. I will never forget the sight of the neighborhood kids crying and rolling on the ground in laughter. But that didn't change how we felt about ourselves. We were so convinced from my dad's prep talk that we held our heads high, put those homemade skates on, and rode them until the wheels fell off. When they laughed, we just reminded them of what our dad said: "You're just jealous."

Once they realized they couldn't upset us, make us feel bad, or stop us from having fun and riding our unique skates, they started asking if they could try them out. We were always taught to share, so we were happy to share. It brought us all together in a sense. The differences that remained between us were null and void because we all found something that everyone could equally enjoy, and we did just that. It took wisdom for my dad to bring us together and make everybody forget about status and just enjoy each other's company. This was one of the most joyous moments of my childhood.

My dad had the same way with grown folks that he had with kids. If he discerned that someone needed encouragement, he would eagerly snap into comedian mode, and the laughter would just begin. If a married couple was having issues and he was called to counsel them, his wisdom allowed him to create a way to make them laugh and forget they were ever upset. My dad had a way of making people see things from a different perspective.

Foundations Create Generations

My mom was raised with both of her parents and was accustomed to a different way of living. She was born in North Carolina and came to Michigan when she was three years old. Both of her parents were from North Carolina. After moving to Michigan, they would go back and visit at least once a year.

My mom was from a large family and had five brothers and one sister. They were only able to afford the bare necessities. My mom's father, Herman Ledwell, whom I affectionately called Paw Paw, was the sole provider in the household. My granny (Margaret) stayed home and took care of the family. Granny was fearful and never got her driver's license, so she depended on Paw Paw when she needed to go anywhere.

My mom was unique. On one hand, she was passive, sensitive, and tender in nature growing up. Because she was the only girl for nine years, she was spoiled rotten, and she wasn't afraid to say what was on her mind. My mom was also creative. Her hands were anointed. She did everything from sewing our clothes as small children and decorating countless weddings, receptions, and anniversary parties to making custom drapes out of used sheets she bought from the local thrift stores. My mom could create anything. I believe she had the gift of healing in her hands.

My mom was raised in a Christian home and was taught the church of God doctrine. I remember my mom expressing that my granny never told her that she loved her when she was a little girl. My mom thought that maybe granny didn't know how to verbally communicate her love since her mother died when she was just three years old. My mom often shared stories with me about being molested by a close family friend when she was a little girl, and it caused her to be fearful. She shared with me in detail that this family friend had a few kids of his own, so he would frequently offer to take her to the park to play with his kids. Since my granny had so many kids, she welcomed the invitation. Once he had permission to take her, he would drop his kids off and take my mom to isolated locations and perform inappropriate sexual acts. These encounters were the root of the fear my mom carried with her throughout her entire life. She never liked being alone. She was easily startled, and it didn't take much to make her cry.

My dad and mom first met at Eastern Junior High School and later became high school sweethearts. After high school, and with a year or two of college under their belts, my parents left home and got married. My father was twenty-two and mother was nineteen. My dad was hired into the local General Motors plant, and they bought their first house on a small dead-end street in Pontiac, Michigan, a small city thirty minutes north of Detroit, Michigan.

I was born a year after they got married. My mom was so excited when I was born that she would sit for hours and play with my fingers, toes, and hair as if she was playing with a baby doll. She didn't work at the time, so she stayed home and poured all of her love and affection into me.

It wasn't long before I had a little company because my sister, Wanda, was born only eighteen months after me. Wanda was my first best friend. My mom said I thought Wanda was my baby instead of hers. She required lots of attention because she was sickly early on. My mom had her hands full. Although Wanda's role as my playmate had not begun, I was overjoyed to have someone to occupy my time. Because she was new at being a mom, she needed help and frequently visited my granny's house for a break. My mom made sure to tell me how important I was for being the big sister and such a big helper.

I didn't learn until much later that my house was full of valuable and precious things. My mom was an intercessor. She would go to war in the spirit on the behalf of others. She had been interceding for me all of my life. The enemy has been on an assignment to destroy my life from the time I was conceived.

My mom told me a story of an incident that happened while she was pregnant with me. One day, she was shopping at a local store, and a man walked up to her and punched her in the stomach. She wasn't sure why, but she knew from the beginning there was an attack on the seed she was carrying.

When I was a little girl, I remember her telling me that God told her, "The enemy is after the seed that is inside of this child." As a child, I didn't understand this. It took many years before I knew exactly what it meant. The truth is that there is something great and powerful about me that I just didn't know. I'm reminded that a thief only comes after things of value, and a thief would never rob an empty house. The Bible refers to the devil as a thief. John 10:10 (NIV) says, "The thief comes only to steal and kill and destroy...."

Merging Foundations

My dad and mom loved God so much. Much of their time was spent at church. Their duties increased after Pastor Williams and his wife passed away. Some years later, my dad's oldest brother, Chester Hendon Sr., became our pastor. Deliverance Mission Apostolic Faith wasn't just a church; it was a family. We did everything from eat to vacation together. The teachings were strict, and the women were only allowed to wear dresses. Women wearing pants was forbidden and considered worldly.

My dad worked hard to help Uncle Chester with the ministry. My dad was responsible for opening and locking up the church before and after services, he played the drums, was a Sunday school teacher, preacher, collected the offering, cut the grass, cleaned the church, and anything else he could get busy doing for God.

Although she did not like being the center of attention, my mom was also a Sunday school teacher. She sang in the choir and made the robes for the children's choir, and she was a minister's wife. Being a minister's wife, mom and dad occasionally had to counsel married couples, administer activities for the children's ministry, and be on time. This was funny because anybody who knew my mom knew she was never on time for anything.

After serving faithfully in multiple capacities, my dad became a powerful and anointed minister. He was so powerful that churches all over the state would invite him to come and preach. Sometimes, he would preach at revivals that lasted a week long. My dad was a threat to the enemy's kingdom. With my parents being so busy with ministry, there just wasn't time for anything except church. The house was always a mess, and there was no order or structure. This is why balance is so important and something I've always struggled with.

I believe my parents touched so many people over the years of ministry and fellowship. They did their best and had a genuine heart to serve God. But while they were busy with all the responsibilities that came along with their roles in the ministry, the devil was busy too. When the devil couldn't defeat them in one area, he tried to attack them in another area. The generational pattern of fear was growing. My granny walked in fear, and so did my mom. And now that demon of fear was on assignment to claim me too.

Tracing Roots of Fear

The enemy came against me at an early age and began to plant many seeds to destroy me. The first seed was fear. The assignment of fear is to cripple you and prevent you from moving forward in your destiny. The crippling from fear operates in the same way as a person with no legs. Maybe that's where the term "crippled with fear" comes from. Fear keeps you from walking out your full potential. It keeps you from seeing things clearly and will silence the beautiful possibilities that you dream about.

I remember so vividly the day fear gripped my life. I was around four years old. I went to the bathroom as usual, but this time, I was terrified. When I sat down on the toilet seat to use the bathroom, a frog was in the toilet. The frog jumped, and so did I. I remember being so afraid that when I screamed, no sound came out of my mouth. This experience caused me to have problems sleeping and wetting the bed. This continued throughout adolescence.

Fear became a part of my daily routine. The generational pattern of fear continued. My mom's life was consumed by it, and now, here I was fighting the same demon. The fear battle is real. When you don't fight against the spirit of fear, you nurture it instead. Generational curses are passed down as a result of rebellion against God. Rebellion is simply not doing it the way you are told to. This is why reading the Word of God is important because we can find specific information concerning everything we encounter. This behavior must be corrected, or it just spreads like a virus and continues to become an endless cycle. Before you know it, fear bleeds into areas of your life that had nothing to do with what caused you fear in the first place. Since my granny walked in some level of fear, then I can trace the fear that my mom walked in. Since my mom walked in fear, I can trace the fear I walked in.

I've learned over the years that the enemy doesn't play fair, and he comes in the early stages of development to plant seeds of destruction before you even have an opportunity to understand the magnitude of what's happening to you. Years later, I began to take a deeper look into the spiritual interpretation of frogs. A book by Ira L. Milligan documented that the Frog Spirit was a demon and represented witchcraft and curses. She associated the frog with "…evil words (as in "casting a spell"); puffed up." The Bible speaks of frogs being associated with unclean spirits.

Revelation 16:13 says, "And I saw three unclean spirits like frogs come out of the mouth of the dragon, and out of the mouth of the beast, and out of the mouth of the false prophet."

Psalm 78:45 records, "He sent divers sorts of flies among them, which devoured them; and frogs, which destroyed them."

My mom, the intercessor, described the attacks against me as spiritual warfare. She recalls being asleep and not being able to wake up. My mom could hear the sound of demons dragging chains down the hallway. The demons would come to my room as I slept, and my mom would plead the blood of Jesus until they would leave. The demons would leave my room and come to where my mom was sleeping. The demons would breath hard and touch my mom inappropriately to make their intentions known and reveal their true identity. She couldn't scream, and she couldn't move. They were on assignment to sexually attack me as I slept, but my mom was an intercessor. She was determined that this type of demonic activity would not happen on her watch. My mom was fighting a spiritual battle and trying to use natural, physical weapons.

According to Britannica, Incubus is described as a "demon in male form that seeks to have sexual intercourse with sleeping women." The female version of this demon is called Succubus.

During these encounters of spiritual warfare, if you are not spiritually mature, trained, and equipped, you become prey to these demonic spirits. In 2 Corinthians 2:10–11, the Bible warns us to not be ignorant of the devil's devices. This is one of the ways we allow the enemy access to our life and goods. The Word of God gives instructions on how to overcome the devil in Ephesians 6:10–17:

"Finally, my brethren, be strong in the Lord, and in the power of his might. Put on the whole armour of God, that ye may be able to stand against the wiles of the devil. For we wrestle not against flesh and blood, but against principalities, against powers, against the rulers of the darkness of this world, against spiritual wickedness in high places. Wherefore take unto you the whole armour of God, that ye may be able to withstand in the evil day, and having done all, to stand. Stand therefore, having your loins girt about with truth, and having on the breastplate of righteousness; And your feet shod with the preparation of the gospel of peace; Above all, taking the shield of faith, wherewith ye shall be able to quench all the fiery darts of the wicked. And take the helmet of salvation, and the sword of the Spirit, which is the word of God...."

My mom had not been trained or reached a level of spiritual maturity in this area, so in some areas, it caused her to respond naturally, not spiritually. Whenever encountering a demonic spirit, if you plan to conquer it, you must do it God's way. Not doing it God's way opens the door for more spirits to overtake you. Demonic spirits that are not dealt with properly according to the Word of God causes generational curses.

Before I was mature enough to understand my family demons, I was already fighting them. When the devil couldn't win in this area of sexual attack early in my life, he used other methods to plant seeds of destruction. I believe my experience with the frog was the root of where my fear began. Anything that brings you fear is not of God. Paul said in 2 Timothy 1:7, "For God hath not given us the spirit of fear; but of power, and love, and of a sound mind." Fear does not just show up and manifest from situations. Fear can also be adopted through the voice of influence. Being surrounded by others who are fearful can also cause you to be fearful if you are not rooted in God's Word.

Faith is the opposite of fear, and to battle fear, you must have faith. Hebrews 11:6 says, "But without faith it is impossible to please God." From this, you can see how walking in fear keeps you from pleasing God. With all of the negative things that fear produces, I challenge you to search areas in your life where fear has crept in. If fear has taken root and caused you to not walk in the freedom that God intended for you to access, faith is the prescription and cure.

Reflection Questions

1. When did you first encounter fear?

2. Can you identify any areas where fear has kept you from functioning?

3. How does the Bible instruct us to overcome fear? (Read Psalms 34:4-5, 1 John 4:18, Psalms 23:4, Mathew 8:25-27, Luke1:12-14, and Luke 1:29-31)

CHAPTER 2
Confusion

With two small babies and the demand of responsibilities from the ministry, my mom needed lots of help. Because she didn't usually work, she would occasionally pick up a job just long enough to get a big-ticket item that she didn't want to ask my dad to buy. This began a habit of me being left with various people.

My parent's heart to serve God caused them to allow a homeless lady to stay in our home for an extended amount of time. When the lady first moved in, my mom gave her two rules: don't go in her bedroom for any reason and don't have sex with her husband. Their intention was to help guide her in the right direction, but this arrangement just opened another door for the enemy to enter in. I remember being in my room at night listening through the thin walls of our small fragile house. My parents never fought in front of me, but I could hear the faint arguments and conversations from their bedroom. Their arguments were typically about the lack of sex in their marriage. This became a regular issue in their marriage for years to come.

Because my mom was molested and never dealt with it, she developed a negative perspective about sex and intimacy. I remember her saying that she really didn't like sex and would prefer not to be intimate because it reminded her of her childhood abuser.

When a child is robbed of their innocence, their mind needs to process not only what has happened but also why it has happened. When the mind is left with nothing to satisfy the intellect, it disturbs the soul. As a result, every area of a victim's life mirrors their offense. Owning the role of a victim becomes their position when the proper steps aren't taken to heal. Subconsciously, the person believes they did something to provoke or warrant the offense. Victims usually put more emphasis on how they feel about what happened instead of steps and solutions on healing and becoming a survivor. The difference between a victim and a survivor is just a matter of perspective. This is why healing is so important.

Childhood sexual abuse is a real issue, and when it's not addressed in a healthy manner, it causes problems in adulthood in the area of intimacy. Marriage is designed for intimacy, and anyone who has issues in this area is opening the door for destruction in their marriage. Self-esteem, confidence, and self-worth take a huge blow behind the scenes of a childhood sexual abuse victim. How can a person who has a wounded mentality partake in such a vulnerable activity? Marriage requires trust, sacrifice, and being vulnerable. When you ignore, cover up, or deny sexual issues, they can resurface later in other areas of your life. You unknowingly invite this dysfunction into your life, and the intimacy of marriage becomes a burden instead of a God-ordained blessing.

If you are a victim of childhood sexual abuse, it is important to seek therapy. Therapy helps you sort through negative thoughts associated with the abuse. In addition to having a support system, therapy helps you to learn a new perspective about your pain and provides a healthy outlet during healing. Trust me, with the right help, you can see yourself as a survivor.

Bitterness Has a Beginning

Our new visitor was a drug addict and wasn't honest about her lifestyle. When my parents left for work, she would take me to the dope house. It was a dark and dingy place. We lived on a dead end street, so we took a shortcut to the dead end of the block and walked to a housing project. I was so afraid because it smelled awful, and I didn't know any of these strange people. But I quickly got used to my new routine.

Once we were inside, the curtains stayed closed, and the lighting was always dim. There was a distinct smell that I had never smelled before. I later learned that it was the smell of crack cocaine. I had no idea where I was. I remember it being broad daylight outside, but when you walk inside and close the door, it was like you were in another world.

The lady who took me there would disappear as soon as we hit the door and wouldn't show up until it was time for us to leave. There were other adults there, but I didn't know any of them. They seemed nice at first by offering me snacks and friendly small talk, making sure to tell me each time I visited how beautiful I was as if it were a prerequisite. They were doing all sorts of things to perfect the atmosphere they worked so hard to create. Playing cards, dominoes, and dice was a regular activity. Music was always playing like it was a party.

A trip to the bathroom turned into me passing by rooms that were demonstrating all kinds of demonic activity. One room had people smoking and drinking while listening to music. Another room was being used for sexual activity. And the last room I remember was where the drug deals were being conducted.

This experience was hard for me to process as a kid. I would stay in the bathroom until someone would need to use it. I calmed myself by playing in the water because water is soothing to me. If I wasn't in the bathroom, I was sitting in either the living room or the kitchen with some stranger's hands in my panties. This was the first time I was touched inappropriately in a sexual manner. I was shaking in my seat, but I didn't utter a single word. All the while, my babysitter was somewhere in the house getting high.

The first time this happened, I thought to myself, I'm never coming here ever again. I didn't understand that I wasn't in control of any decisions, and my next visit was predicated on my mom needing a babysitter. I knew when my mom went to work, I would be left in the babysitters care again, so I couldn't dare tell anyone what was happening to me. I can remember the feeling of knowing something wasn't right and couldn't figure out why these things were never done to me at home. With every return visit, I was sure to catch someone's attention only to end up with someone touching me inappropriately again.

Meanwhile, my dad and mom's sexual issues opened a door, and at some point, my dad gave in to the temptation from his sexual neglect and had an affair with the babysitter. I remember my mom crying for what seemed like an eternity. She said she knew something wasn't right when she found the babysitter's hair in her bedroom. She managed to break both of the rules that my mom gave her to follow.

The Blessing After Bitterness

My mom found out she was pregnant with my baby sister Joy after my dad's infidelity was exposed. My mom cried every day until the doctor told her that she was threatening a miscarriage. She was hurt. It was a deep hurt. The kind of hurt that fractures your soul. My mom refused to name her new beautiful baby, so my dad said her name would be Joy. If you've ever met her, then you know she has the perfect name. She certainly is joy personified.

After Joy was born, my mom battled depression. I remember my mom would let Joy sit for hours and cry. She would secure her in the high chair and start doing chores around the house and let Joy cry like she didn't hear her at all. I'm not sure how much time passed by, but we moved out of that house. My mom said she couldn't live there with those memories, so we moved into another house.

Shortly after we moved, my dad finally got his boy. Jerry Jr. was born, and we've always called him Little Jerry. Everybody was so ecstatic. Since he was the first boy in the family, all of us girls spoiled him rotten and treated him just like he was one of us. We put bows in his hair, let him play with our dolls, painted his fingers and toe nails, and carried him everywhere like his legs were broken. We all absolutely adored little Jerry Jr.

My mom tried really hard to forgive my dad, but she was so hurt from the affair. Although two children were born after the affair, sex remained an issue. Having little Jerry Jr. in a sense helped my mom to function in all of this dysfunction. Jerry Jr. brought so much joy to the household until it was hard to not be happy during this season. My dad was overjoyed to finally have his boy. My mom enjoyed the positive energy and constant excitement coming from all directions.

Church Hurt and the Waves of Abuse

Although our family was experiencing innumerable traumatic events, we were still faithful to our church. We spent most of our time at church. We practically lived there. We were there early in the morning on Sundays and wouldn't be ready to go home until about 8:00 or 9:00 pm. We were back on Tuesday for a prayer meeting. Wednesdays were for Bible class and choir practice along with ministers' training on Fridays. Saturdays were just for cleaning the church. And before you know it, it's Sunday again. I was at the disposal of anyone at church who thought I was adorable, and I was usually the center of attention.

At the age of about eight, I was molested in the church nursery by one of the teenagers who attended our church. He was creepy, and I was so afraid. I couldn't figure out where everybody was and why nobody came looking for me. He had his way with me, and I was left wondering what happened. I felt like what he did wasn't right, but I was just too young to understand. I was also molested by a babysitter that attended our church. She was the babysitter that came to our house and stayed the night when my parents would be out late on school nights. She did things to me that later made me question and struggle with my sexuality.

I was robbed of my innocence, confused, and fearful before I even had my first training bra. I wasn't old enough to understand why a girl would do these kinds of things to me. I wasn't old enough to understand why what she did to me felt good. And I certainly wasn't old enough to know how to separate my feelings from the facts. By this time, I was just completely confused. There is a level of guilt that is indescribable when trying to understand why something so wrong feels so good. Struggling with sexual identity causes you to reject the people and things designed for your life. You waste time searching for the right things in the wrong places. Sexual identity is a real issue that many people suffer from. I was confused because I had been robbed of my innocence by both genders.

Other than church, I spent a lot of time at my granny's house. My mom loved it there because she was afraid of being home alone while my dad was away working. Granny had five boys and two girls, so she kept a full house.

Her house was a place where the adults never really watched the kids and lots of unfortunate things happened there. The house my granny lived in was a big two family flat. The adults occupied the main floor, and the children occupied the upstairs. The adults rarely would come upstairs for anything at all. I was molested so many times there that it practically became the norm. Although granny's house was a fun place to be, my confusion deepened, and I became numb. I stopped trying to even figure out why these things were happening.

There was something common between all of the people who touched me inappropriately: they all told me they loved me and cared about me. So, I became extremely confused. I began to believe the reason these things happened to me was because I was beautiful. I determined in my mind that I would do everything I could to not be beautiful in hopes that maybe it would stop happening. I became a tomboy. I stopped washing up to smell bad on purpose and took little care in my appearance. It didn't help at all. In fact, it increased. I became angry every time someone referred to me as beautiful. It was a constant reminder of why I was a target. I didn't want to wear dresses anymore because the easy access that came along with it helped all these people to take advantage of me. It got old real quick, and I promised when I was old enough to make my own decisions that I would never wear another dress again in my life.

I'm the oldest child, so I've always been taught to be the bigger person, to be responsible for my siblings, and that I was too big for kid stuff. In a sense, I do feel like I never had a childhood because I was robbed of so much so early. Being a little girl is a huge deal. Everybody fusses over little girls being clean, having their hair done, nail polish, lip gloss, ribbons, lace, playing dress up, and all kinds of things. Little girls grow into women who have babies and teach them the same things they learned.

Growing up, I never wanted to have kids because I was too afraid of what may happen to them when I wasn't around. Just like my parents weren't around when terrible things happened to me. It was their job to know everything about me. It was their job to keep me away from places that would strip me of my innocence. My dad and mom's busy schedule didn't give them a free pass to ignore all the things I was experiencing. The fact that they didn't know made no difference to me because I was hurting and needed somebody to blame. I still held resentment in my heart toward my parents, even though they didn't know. They were both prime candidates for blame as far as I was concerned.

Misunderstood

The baggage I was carrying by the time I reached my teenage years was unreal. Everywhere I went, people judged me without knowing what things I had to fight through. They judged my attitude and my lack of ability to move forward. This is when I got the reputation of being just down right mean, promiscuous, and crazy. Word curses are powerful and can damage a person who doesn't know who they are.

I didn't care what anybody called me as long as nobody touched me again. I couldn't trust anybody. My innocence was taken, I didn't want to be beautiful, but I had to keep wearing those dresses. I was in a dilemma, and I just didn't think I was loved at all. I realize now that this was a lie that the enemy wanted me to believe. How could anybody love somebody and do these terrible things? Although my parents weren't aware of all these secrets, I was convinced that they didn't love me either because they were nowhere around to protect me when these things happened to me.

According to the Rape, Abuse & Incest National Network, the nation's largest anti-sexual violence organization, "…every nine minutes, child protective services substantiates or finds evidence for a claim of child sexual abuse." They also document that 1 in 9 girls and 1 in 53 boys under the age of eighteen experience sexual abuse or assault at the hands of an adult. In 88% of the sexual abuse claims, the perpetrator is male. About 9% of cases are female. They record that 82% of all victims under eighteen are female. Females ages sixteen to nineteen are four times more likely than the general population to be victims to mental health challenges. Victims are about four times more likely to develop symptoms of drug abuse, about four times more likely to experience post-traumatic stress disorder, and about three times more likely to experience a major depressive episode as adults.

Mayoclinic.org documents the many different symptoms of child abuse. Their research found that "A child who is being abused may feel guilty, ashamed or confused. He or she may be afraid to tell anyone about the abuse, especially if the abuser is a relative or family friend." They list a variety of red flags to look for such as withdrawal from friends or usual activities. Changes in behavior such as aggression, anger, hostility, hyperactivity, changes in school performance, depression, anxiety or unusual fears, a sudden loss of self-confidence, rebellious or defiant behavior, or self-harm or suicide attempts are among the symptoms and red flags.

Children need to feel a sense of trust and security in order for them to have the confidence to share such huge secrets. When a child feels overlooked and neglected, they aren't able to develop a strong sense of trust and protection as a result. Parents who develop a strong communication relationship with their child/children are more likely to increase the chances of the child feeling safe enough to share such enormous information. It is safe to say that trust is the major component that allows a child to feel safe enough to release without punishment or penalty resulting in more shame and condemnation. Children are born innocent and with great potential. The value of an innocent child and their potential is usually the responsibility of the person who created them.

However, children are often left to be raised by someone other than the person who should have been responsible. When the responsibility of value is dismissed, innocence begins to diminish and takes on a new form. Every future possibility is jeopardized when any child is not valued. When a child's value and innocence are not protected, it changes the entire course of that child's life. Broken children become broken adults.

It took me many years of therapy to overcome the abuse. I had to dig deep in the depths of my soul to find things that I didn't know I had, like strength and courage. If I stayed the way I was, I wouldn't have allowed myself the opportunity to find out if I could be healed and whole. What about my gifts and talents that I forfeited? What about all the great dreams I gave up on? Overcoming abuse causes you to soul search. It is important to find a safe place to heal not just physically but also mentally. I needed God's love to survive.

The first thing I had to do was determine if I was going to stay a victim or fight to become a survivor. Overcoming abuse required me to abort every thought that told me I was responsible for what happened to me. In order to receive the love I was longing for, I had to let go of all the emotions associated with not being loved. Learning to love myself also helped me to love and appreciate others.

Reflection Questions

1. Have you experienced difficulty receiving love from others because of past hurt?

2. Do you have compassion for others who battle the same areas you have overcome?

3. Does changing your perspective about something help you to process it differently?

CHAPTER 3
Desperate for Love

By the time I became a teenager, I was confused, angry, disappointed, and filled with hate. I was considered a troubled teen and was difficult to handle at school. I was told everything I couldn't do but not what I could do or what possibilities were attainable for me. Up until this point, I had an encounter with fear from the frog experience. I'd been mishandled by the babysitter who left me with strangers in a crack house, and I had been molested at church and at granny's house. Needless to say, I had trust issues.

Being raised in a strict Christian household, I felt like a caged animal. The appropriate milestones for growth were void. I wasn't introduced to womanhood through a conversation, but I encountered the experience through a visit to a public restroom. Boys and sex were forbidden conversations, and I wasn't allowed to go anywhere or do anything. The neighborhood kids had the type of freedoms that I dreamed of. They went to the movies, to the mall, to the skating rink, to teen parties but I wasn't allowed to go to any of those places. I felt like an outcast. This made me want to sneak and do things because I knew that was the only way I would be able to. Being deprived of the good life shaped my decisions, and I wanted to experience everything that was being kept from me. I'm sure this sounds pretty extreme, but it's true. Thirst comes from deprivation, and I was thirsty.

All I wanted was freedom and love. I wanted it so bad that I could taste it. My mom exhausted her patience with me. So, my dad was the disciplinary of the household, and he did not spare the rod. I was a daddy's girl. My dad wanted a son so bad, but since he didn't get his boy until later, I became his surrogate son.

One time, my dad took me fishing, and I caught my first fish. I got so excited when I got a bite on my pole that I jerked the pole with force. When my dad took the fish off my line and its mouth was crooked, my dad laughed until he cried. Another fond memory is when my dad took me to target practice in the woods with him and his buddies. He gave me his shotgun and asked me to try and shoot the cans off the wooden tree stumps about 25 feet away. The force of the gun would knock me on my hind parts, that's what my dad called it, and he got an absolute kick out of this each and every time. We would high five, and he would brag to his friends that I was his big girl.

With all the dysfunction I was having, I was guaranteed to be on his radar constantly. My parents couldn't figure out the cause of my behavior. I became rebellious and angry. I started stealing anytime we visited a store. I was a class clown at school, which contributed to me being in detention more than I was in class. I failed early in junior high school and ended up in the same class as my younger sister Wanda. I started sneaking to hang out with boys, which was absolutely forbidden.

I felt numb from all the sexual abuse, but the whippings I got from my dad were evidence that I still had feelings. I can remember how bad those whippings were. When my dad got a hold of me, I wanted to see Jesus every time. Because if anybody could help me escape my dad's punishment, I knew that only Jesus could.

Now, it's funny to actually rehearse these memories because it certainly wasn't funny then. It seemed like I got a whipping every day. My siblings were so accustomed to me getting in trouble that when they misbehaved, I quickly became their saving grace. To escape my dad's wrath, they would say, "Keshia did it." They frequently lied on me to get out of being disciplined. For years, I took the whippings for the team, but once I moved out of the house, they were exposed. But that didn't stop them from blaming me when they were in a tight spot.

After fourteen years of marriage, my parents divorced. Their ministry at Deliverance Mission Apostolic Faith Church ended, and they were left with so much hurt and shame. Because my parents were leaders in the church, their divorce had a huge negative impact on those they frequently fellowshipped with. All kinds of gossip and negative rumors were being spread. This kept my parents from church to avoid the negative gossip. Many people find it difficult to move past the things that have hurt or cause them pain. When your conversation always finds a way to reintroduce your offense or offender, then you haven't let go or forgiven. The practice of forgiveness can't be applied if vindication is more important than victory.

The problem with walking in offense is that it blinds the eyes. Offense blocks the offended from being able to see the offenses they cause others. This is also an endless cycle that will guarantee a bitter heart instead of a breakthrough. When unforgiveness and bitterness is nurtured, it births a prideful spirit and perception. I've learned that pride operates just like a thief. Pride robs you of the ability to forgive. Forgiveness requires a humble heart, not a prideful one.

After careful observation from adolescence to adulthood, I can conclude that when you don't forgive or speak about people in a negative way, it keeps you in bondage and lack. When you choose to forgive and speak well of others even when they speak poorly of you, favor, grace, and blessings overtake different areas of your life.

I learned some of the traits I inherited from my mom. She was opinionated, and so was I. She had no filter, and neither did I. My mom had the gift of healing in her hands, and so do I. My mom had the gift of prophecy along with the discerning of spirits, and so do I. Because I was the oldest child and came just a year after my parents were married, I have memories that my siblings were not old enough to recall or process. As I began to look at myself, I noticed several things that made me different from my siblings. They all seemed normal, and I was dysfunctional. I didn't have a big brother or big sister, and they did. I have several allergies to foods, and they don't have any. I wasn't given a middle name, and my siblings have middle names. I was sexually abused all my life, and I wasn't aware of anything like that happening to any of them. Not that I would have felt better or wanted anything to happen to them. But I was comparing to find out what made me so different from them.

I later learned that the difference between my siblings and I was just a matter of purpose and destiny. Each individual person has their own unique journey. Each person's journey is tailor made and designed by God for their specific purpose. My journey was different because my purpose is different. It took many years before I learned this, so I struggled with comparing myself to others until I matured into this mindset.

Nothing good comes from comparison unless you are the only subject. Comparison of others becomes dangerous because the foundations are never certain. People compare others based on their perception. Perception forms the opinion, and the opinion creates a judgment. Comparison keeps you in a mindset of division. Comparison robs you of being uniquely creative without judgment. Matthew 7:5 refers to a person who walks in judgment of others and compares themselves to others as a hypocrite.

A New Normal

Since my parents were now divorced, my mom had no time to look after us. My mom had to find a way to support herself, so she became a working woman. This gave me the freedom that I longed for. My dad wasn't in the home anymore, and the divorce was so bitter that we didn't see my dad much during this time. My dad was homeless and lived in his vehicle for a year, and then he got his first apartment. My mom remained in the family house that we were raised in.

I remember my dad telling my mom after the divorce, "Keshia will be pregnant soon if you don't get her under control." While my mom was working, there were no rules or restrictions. I felt like the caged animal had been let out to play. I started having lots of boy company, and home seemed more like a cool place. As a result, I became pregnant with my first child at the age of fifteen. My dad was right, and my mom was both hurt and disappointed in me. I felt like poison to my siblings, and I knew for sure that absolutely nobody on this earth understood what mental and emotional state of mind I was in.

Although I was already a huge disappointment, being a pregnant teen brought a whole new level of shame, but I was willing to endure the shame in order to find the love I was so desperately seeking. My pregnancy made me examine myself even closer. I concluded that I needed to find out who I was and fast. I was going to be a mom.

I promised I would love and protect my baby and would never let anyone do to my child what all those people did to me. I felt cursed, and in my mind, the only way to reverse the curse was to have a baby and give it all of my love. In some twisted way, my mind convinced me that I could change some of the broken parenting methods I felt like my parents practiced in raising me, even though I was still broken with the wrong perspective. I felt so unworthy of love, so this baby was just what I needed. So I thought.

I named my first-born Chris Jr. after his dad, Chris Anthony Cann. We called him Little Chris and called his dad Big Chris. I was super excited to have someone to finally love me for me.

I met my son's father through my next door neighbor, and we became good friends. I felt like Big Chris was just the friend I needed after all I had been through. He was kind of shy, but he was a total gentleman. He wasn't aggressive and never abusive, so that was a plus. Big Chris was funny and thoughtful, and he was my new best friend. We went everywhere together. We got a summer job together at one of the local middle school summer programs.

When we found out I was pregnant, we were both super excited. One of my most memorable moments of my pregnancy was when Big Chris took me on a shopping spree in Canada. He bought everything we needed for our new baby. We had diapers stacked all up the side of the wall in my bedroom that I shared with my sister Wanda. The dresser was decorated neatly with all the items we could think our baby would need. Preparing for my pregnancy and having a baby resulted in me overcrowding my sister's space in the room we shared.

The house was really crowded now because my mom announced she was also pregnant. My mom had a gorgeous baby boy seven months after I did and named him Ryan. When my mom first announced she was pregnant, she wasn't married or in a relationship, so she would often refer to Ryan as her "oops baby." When my mom told me she was pregnant, we cried together. My mom was feeling the same shame that I was feeling. My mom was still trying to recover from her childhood abuse, church hurt, and fourteen-year failed marriage, and now a brand new baby was on the way. This season brought many changes.

I had no idea that this was a fantasy and parenthood was a real thing with real issues. Parenthood is for the mature, not for kids, but it didn't matter to me. I was determined to have someone to love and someone who would love me right back. I found out quickly how playing house was dangerous, and without being responsible, I was in trouble.

With tensions high, I left home soon after my baby boy was born. Big Chris was new at parenthood and was excited to be a new dad, so my son spent most of the time with him. It worked out well because I didn't have anywhere to go and was hoping around from house to house until I wore out my welcome and eventually ended up homeless. Leaving home and getting my freedom was number one on my list of priorities, but liberation comes with a price.

The combination of being thirsty for freedom and being promiscuous got the best of me. I was out of the house and could go anywhere and do anything I wanted to do. I wasn't honest with Big Chris and started lying about where I was and who I was with. We ended our relationship but vowed to be friends for life since we were better at being friends than being exclusive. Big Chris always took good care of our son, and I never had anything to worry about when it came to him providing for him. But I still needed somebody to love me, so I was on a mission.

Trading Rebellion for Bondage

When I first left home and broke up with Big Chris, I rekindled a relationship with my first love who was my childhood friend. Everybody from the neighborhood knew that Charles (Chuck) Brown and Keshia Hendon would be together forever. He was a hustler, but he described himself as a survivor. We lived in his car at the time while he was in the streets making money. This was so much fun to me because I had never experienced such freedom. I asked him if he could teach me what he was doing so we both could make some money. His response was absolutely not. As someone who was raised a church girl, I never had any experience with the streets. His lifestyle intrigued me, and I was going to try anything I thought I was big and bad enough to do.

Since Chuck wasn't willing to teach me, I found another guy from the neighborhood and asked him to teach me how to hustle and get some money. Rebellion was in full operation by this time because I had no accountability anywhere. Unforgiveness and bitterness had taken root. My new friend's name was Robert Webster, but his family and friends called him Robbie. When Chuck found out I hooked up with Robbie against his wishes, he blew a gasket, and we broke up. So much for together forever. Our lives went in different directions, but we remained friends.

I was now left with nowhere to go, and Robbie ended up letting me come and live with him. He was staying with his mother at the time, but she didn't mind him having company or moving me in. That was something I wasn't used to. Their house was unorganized just like mine was, so I was right at home. I was willing to do anything as long as I didn't have to go back to my mom's house. I was finally free. I could come and go as I pleased with no accountability.

When I first met Robbie, it was great because we weren't a couple. We were making lots of money. Eating good, drinking good, and wearing nice clothes became the focal point of our intentions. Things were going well, so we became intimate and agreed to get married. We were making so much money that we moved out of his mom's house and got our own place together. After we got married, he became abusive immediately and displayed lots of insecurities. This was the start of a downward spiral of depression.

Robbie was an alcoholic and got violent after drinking. The police were called to our apartment on numerous occasions and several police reports were filed. The police were so used to being called to my residence they would patrol past my house on a regular basis. I became friends with police officers by being promiscuous. My dad and Uncle Chester would frequently take their lunch breaks from the plant nearby to visit and keep me company. I was so excited every time they came by. In a sense, I felt protected for the short time they were visiting.

This marriage produced baby number two. Shavonne Marie Webster was my first beautiful baby girl. All I wanted was to be loved. My son still spent most of his time with his dad while I tried to make my marriage work. Being a new wife and mother was a battle for me. My baby girl would scream, and I couldn't figure out how to settle her down. I would feed her and change her diaper, and she would just cry. I would give her a bath and make her smell good, and she would still cry. Her dad would pick her up, and she would get quiet right away.

One time, I remember being home alone, and I couldn't get her to stop crying. So, I put her on the sofa and sat on the floor. The sound of her screaming drove me crazy, and I had a crazy thought to put my baby in the dryer and cover her with clothes until I couldn't hear her anymore. This thought scared me so bad because I didn't want to hurt my baby. I needed my baby for the love I was still searching for. I didn't trust myself. I had just been through too much. I wasn't mature enough to be a mom. I would rather leave her than to hurt her. I wasn't sure if I was having these crazy thoughts because I was having a nervous breakdown or if I was so tired of getting physically abused by her dad.

After a while, the abuse and motherhood became unbearable, and I began to look for a way out. I knew that I had to go, so I left my baby with Robbie and moved to Indiana to attend Job Corps, hoping to get a break from the madness. My baby girl was probably seven or eight months old at the time. I told myself I was doing something positive since I became a high school dropout between baby number one and baby number two. The Job Corps wasn't what I expected at all, and the experience was short-lived. After returning home from Job Corp my marriage was coming to an end. I was only married eighteen months before I ended up in divorce court. I wanted love so bad. I listened for it, I looked for it, I gave my body for it, but I couldn't find it to save my life.

After the divorce, I became out of control and started drinking heavily. I began to give my body to anybody I thought would love me.

Hatred Is Cancerous

Shortly after my divorce, I did a follow-up visit with the gynecologist, and I was told I had an abnormal pap smear and would have to come back for further testing. They found cancer cells growing in my cervix, and this began a deep depression. My two kids were now three and four years old, and I asked both of their dads if they would take full permanent custody. I was very sick and was unable to care for them. They agreed, and I began treatment.

The first step of treatment was an attempt to freeze off the precancerous cells that were growing on my cervix. This procedure is called cryosurgery. Freezing gas in the form of liquid nitrogen was used. The cryosurgery procedure didn't work because the cancer cells grew back. Chemotherapy was the next step. This season of my life was so scary, and I felt so alone. I wasn't close to my family during this time because of my life choices. Newly divorced and still very young, I met Amil Robinson, aka Mike Robinson. I thought he was the man of my dreams, but our relationship turned out to be a nightmare. He was mature and taught me so many destructive things. He saw right away how naïve and vulnerable I was, and that is what I believe attracted me to him.

After settling down with him and getting our own apartment, we begin our life together. I got pregnant almost right away, and one abortion after another was our method of birth control. Once we both had a steady job, we decided to keep the next baby, and that gave me hope again. On January 30, 1993, I birthed a baby boy and named him Little Mike Robinson. He was born at 4:10 pm. He had black hair and weighed in at 15.2 oz. His time on earth was short. Little Mike never opened his eyes, so no eye color was documented. He wasn't even a pound, but the hospital representative came to my room to answer any questions I may have had. She explained to me that according to the law, if a baby is born over a certain weight limit, it has to be properly disposed of by a funeral home. This broke my heart because I envisioned them putting my baby in a bag and throwing him in the garbage. Of course, this wasn't the case, but as a young immature girl, that's all I could see.

I wanted to do the right thing for my baby, so I requested the hospital chaplain from the Department of Ministerial Healing to come and pay me a visit. When he arrived, he was a soft-spoken gentleman and asked me if I wanted prayer. I thought, Yes, please. That's why I called you. He offered words of encouragement and invited other hospital volunteers and staff to come in my room for support. Everyone in the room all witnessed the naming ceremony and baptism for Little Mike Robinson. I was given a naming ceremony program tailor made with my baby's name in it. I also received a certificate of baptism. I managed to preserve all of his hospital documents, and I still have a copy of his birth record with his footprints attached.

I remember hearing all the babies crying all the way down the maternity ward. Families were in excitement coming to visit their new bundles of joy, and I had nothing. I had to plan his funeral from my hospital bed, and I wanted to die. The pain was so intense. I wasn't sure if me losing my baby was a result of all those abortions I had. I felt like I was cursed, and I convinced myself that was the reason that my baby died. God knew I didn't need another baby, but I just couldn't understand why every effort I made to get love ended in disappointment.

Baby Devon Is Gone

Out of the hospital and back to work now, I was back on my mission to find love. Shavonne and Chris Jr. seemed to be stable in their environments with their dads, so I just continued my life as if nothing was wrong or dysfunctional, but I was only fooling myself. I missed out on years of valuable time with them because of my immaturity and confusion. Not too long after I got out of the hospital, Amil and I got pregnant again, and this time, I was successful. I had a girl, and she was all mine. Amil named her Porshia Robinson. She wasn't what I wanted, but I needed her to prove I had something of my own to love.

After the pregnancy, Amil grew more abusive. This was the first time that I wanted to go back home, but I knew that wasn't an option. For the first time in my life, I was learning some of the responsibilities of being an adult. Amil taught me lots of valuable things about the real world. Amil was street smart, and his methods were harsh but effective. The problem here was that hurt people, hurt people. During this relationship, I grew tough skin, and being a victim wasn't an option anymore. Although I was still physically there, I would often rehearse how it would feel to be free from all the abuse that went along with staying.

Dreaming was my only way of escape, and I never imagined how I would ever be free again. My whole purpose in leaving home was for love and freedom. Here, I was feeling unloved and bound again. Not facing the real issues from my past proved to deliver a cycle of dysfunction.

One morning, I woke up and found myself in a puddle of blood. Porshia was just a toddler at this time. My sister Wanda rushed me to the hospital, and after a few tests, I was rushed into emergency surgery. I was hemorrhaging and losing blood fast. After surgery, the doctor came out and congratulated me on a successful surgery and a miraculous premature delivery of a baby boy weighing in at only 3lbs and 7oz. I named him Devon Michael Robinson. I was in complete shock because I didn't even know I was pregnant. The doctor came in and asked permission to invite a staff of doctors in to do a study on me and baby Devon. He was born premature at only four months and needed no oxygen or assistance at birth. This was a miracle the doctors said.

Although there was joy in the hospital, there wasn't any joy at home. All of my health issues, limited finances, and the abuse became more intense. I felt the best thing to do was give my baby a good life and not raise another baby in this toxic environment. With the help from a hospital social worker, catholic social services was the agency that assisted with the adoption of my son. The representative came to the hospital, and she was a nice, gentle, and kindhearted lady. She made this difficult process a lot less stressful. My son left the hospital after I signed my parental rights over, and he went to foster care, waiting for the court date of the adoption to be complete.

Adopthelp.com posted an article that stated:
"One of the main reasons that birth mothers choose adoption is because they face financial hardships and may not be able to provide the life they wish for their child...Oftentimes, women parenting other children worry they may not have the financial resources to feed and care for another child. By choosing adoption, birth mothers are ensuring their child will have their basic needs met, as well as many things that she may not have been able to provide, including proper healthcare, education, and access to many more opportunities throughout life."

Adopt Help documents that in their experience, adoption is never selfish. Women who choose to place their baby up for adoption are often selfless, giving, and have such a strong love for their baby that they want what is best for the child. In most cases, they put the needs of the baby before their own desires to parent a child that they may not be able to provide for.

I found this to be interesting so I kept searching for more information. While doing research, I came across an article on adoptionnetwork.com about grieving the loss of a child. They stated the following:

"Placing a child for adoption can cause a sense of loss that is all-encompassing. Describing the birth and actual surrendering of the baby may prompt feelings of numbness, shock, and denial, as well as grief, in the birth parents."

After I was discharged from St. Joseph's Hospital, I never saw baby Devon again. I always had hope that one day I would be reunited with him. This decision shaped my life because although I was still battling depression, this gave me a reason to hold on and not give up.

I've learned to find something that really matters to me when I've experienced these low places of depression. Just like my baby boy, if I give up, I will never afford myself the opportunity to see him again. This concept changed my perception from hurt and loss to hope and wholeness. In a sense, it gave me strength. Having the courage to look forward to something felt better than soaking in sadness. It gave me determination to seek healing for myself so that when I finally meet my son, I will have the strength and energy to love on him from a pure place. But I had to find a way to love myself before any of this could take place.

Reflection Questions

1. What are some of the things that you do or use to fill voids?

2. Can you explain any ways that you may turn your pain into power?

3. How would experiencing a loss change if you knew that you were being set up for something greater?

CHAPTER 4

Forgiveness

I had managed to do almost everything ungodly thus far, and I was feeling pretty useless. I couldn't get anything right. I'm the oldest of four siblings, and the oldest child is supposed to lead by example. Well, I blew that assignment. I did all the things I was taught not to do. I didn't finish high school, I had kids before I was married, and I wasn't on the right path to a good future. I was a baby killer, and the baby I didn't kill I gave away for adoption. I didn't trust where my life was or my ability to provide.

I was depressed, and I became distant with my family and almost never saw any of them. It kept me from sharing life events with family and close friends for the fear of judgment. I told myself I deserved all the bad that happened to me. I built walls, questioned any love that was given, and eventually came to the conclusion that nobody cared about me. I wanted to die, and I would pray every night before I went to sleep, asking God to please not let me wake up in the morning. In my mind, this was proof He wasn't listening since I was still alive. Here I was in pain, still trying to find myself. I was in a constant state of self-analyzing, trying to find out where I went wrong.

I never desired to celebrate my birthday as a kid or an adult until recently. I always thought it was strange that my birthday was on St. Patrick's Day, a day where debauchery and unruliness were celebrated. One year on my birthday, I was taken to a hotel room and abused by a family member, so I've always despised the day I was born. To celebrate my birthday would be like celebrating what happened in that hotel room. It was on my twelfth birthday.

We didn't have much growing up, so birthdays were not extravagant. They were a simple affair. This particular year, a family member asked my mom if they could treat me to a nice birthday. We left my house and headed to a hotel room. I was young, so the ride there seemed far. The place was run down. I was told that my birthday surprise was inside. I went in right away with anticipation of the best birthday ever. When I got inside and the door closed, I looked around for the surprise, but I didn't see anything. So, I sat down on the bed to wait for it to be revealed since it was probably hidden. There was never a birthday surprise. I was the surprise. I remember feeling like such an idiot. I thought, "How could I have been so stupid?" I had been mishandled so many times by the time this happened that I felt like I should have known better.

My birthdays were never the same after that hotel room experience. When I got back home, I went straight to my bedroom. I think I was in shock. I couldn't eat or sleep for days. I developed resentment toward my parents over the years of my childhood. I looked up to them for protection, and I felt like they never protected me. My parents didn't pay attention to the things that were going on all around me. I promised to never be nice anymore. I wanted to be the exact opposite. I wanted to always know what was going on. I wanted to make my own decisions. I didn't want to be weak; I wanted to be strong.

It wasn't until after I had children of my own and all these life experiences that I understood that my parents gave me the best they had to give. My parents did their best raising all of their children. My inability to understand things from a mature perspective kept me in a mindset of looking for someone to blame and hold accountable.

Constantly looking for others to blame and not looking to be accountable to yourself only produces a cycle of judgment. I was never able to receive forgiveness because I wasn't willing to forgive. Mark 11:25–26 says that forgiving others is a prerequisite to your own forgiveness. When Peter asked Jesus how many times we should forgive, Jesus replied by saying, "…seventy times seven" (Matthew 18:21–22). This indicates that we should forgive often, over and over again. This is God's way.

Losing to Win

I'm reminded of all the valleys I've spent my time in, learning valuable lessons. Webster defines a valley as "a low point or condition." Wikipedia characterizes a valley as "…a low area of land between hills or mountains that generally has a river or stream flowing through it." Jesus Christ has been that river flowing through every low place I've traveled. I didn't learn until later that all these things I perceived as negative situations and circumstances were not all from the devil, but some of these things manifested in my life because they were designed to push me into my purpose.

I remember the Lord saying to me, "It is all training for your reigning."

In this life, we are called to endure things that may not feel good at that particular time, but they serve a purpose. In God's timing, we learn that it usually was never about us but rather to help someone else. My mindset during the process of dealing with cervical cancer was toxic. I had no family to support me because I had isolated myself from them. They didn't even know I had gone through that experience until much later.

One day, I was at my granny's house getting my hair pressed. Granny could press my hair better than anyone I knew. She was so good at it that people thought I had a perm when I got out of her chair. Granny didn't play. I'd sit still, and if I didn't want my ear burned, I had to hold it down with my hand.

I wasn't feeling well this particular day, and I remember having a terrible headache. I asked Granny if I could go to the bathroom, and she fussed at me. She told me she didn't have time to be fooling with me, and if I planned on her finishing, I better hurry back. I stood up to go to the bathroom, and I passed out on the floor. When I woke up, I was in St. Joseph's Hospital. This is how my mom learned of my cervical cancer.

Healing and recovering for me looked so different than the other people I saw battling cancer. I would see people cutting their hair off to support their loved ones. I didn't have that type of support, so I was left to deal with my fears, emotions, and struggles alone. I really wasn't alone, but it certainly felt that way. I believed what Deuteronomy 31:6 says: "Be strong and of good courage, fear not, nor be afraid of them: for the LORD thy God, he it is that doth go with thee; he will not fail thee, nor forsake thee."

During this time, I found hope through my church family. Redeemed Christian Center was the place that became my new safe haven. I visited one time, and I knew I was supposed to be there. I quickly became active and joined the auxiliary that seemed most suitable. The praise and worship team was how I first became active because I love to sing. This was the beginning of a positive start for me.

What I learned at my new church was that forgiveness had to come from me first. Others can forgive me, and God can forgive me too, but without me forgiving myself, I would continue to walk in shame from the things of my past. Power is given to whatever you believe. This is why forgiving yourself is so important. Why would anybody do anything for you that you're not willing to do for yourself? Your personal belief causes you to be the first partaker. Actions are shaped by what you believe. Walking in shame keeps you from feeling worthy of forgiveness. Breaking away from the negative behaviors of unforgiveness is difficult but necessary if you plan to heal in those areas. Believing the Word of God will cause you to forgive because you won't be forgiven if you don't offer forgiveness to others.

There are doors in the spiritual realm that we allow to be open when we walk in unforgiveness. Bitterness, resentment, jealousy, bondage, and poor health are just a few. Pride, rebellion, and wanting to be vindicated are a few reasons that prevent people from forgiving others. However, there are benefits to forgiveness. Forgiveness keeps the doors of unforgiveness close. It also keeps you free from the grip of pain from the offense. You choose to demonstrate God's love when you forgive. Besides, the Bible says we should forgive, and there is a reward for our obedience.

I learned through my own trials that love is perfected through the forgiving power of Jesus Christ. Jesus Christ died on the cross so that our sins can be forgiven. When we hold unforgiveness in our hearts, we reject what Jesus Christ did on the cross. Although my life was filled with all these terrible things, there were a few undeniable facts. Everything happens for a reason, and you will never learn what's possible if you give up. Good things can still happen after a loss. Perception changes everything. It's only a loss if you don't learn from it. I believe that there is a purpose for my pain, and it starts with forgiveness. Spirits and generational curses are real, but they can be broken through God's forgiving power. I knew I had to forgive all the people who ever molested, abused, hurt, or talked about me in a negative way.

God's way is always the best way. It always works because He sees the end from the beginning. He is Alpha and Omega in every aspect of life. Even in areas where I'm not able to understand, I must still trust His plan for me. Healing isn't easy, and it's not possible without forgiveness.

Several things needed to happen in order for me to reconcile my past and get free. In the past, forgiveness had been a struggle for me. This is because I've been hurt and mishandled by people close to me all of my life. In order for me to heal, I had to take a look at the areas in my life that still occupied offense and unforgiveness.

First, I needed to identify who my real enemies were so I could protect myself. To me, it didn't make sense to go through this process if I couldn't be wise about who I allowed in my space. I wanted to protect myself from being taken advantage of again, but physical weapons are no good for spiritual battles. The spiritual weapon against offense is forgiveness. Secondly, I had to find a way to build myself up spiritually. This happened by getting more familiar with God's Word and actually believing it.

King David wrote in Psalm 110:1, *"The LORD said unto my Lord, Sit thou at my right hand, until I make thine enemies thy footstool."*

Most people I've heard quote this Scripture have a different perspective than what I understand to be true and effective in my life. I've heard people pray for God to remove their enemies from their space and sometimes from their whole life.

A footstool is a piece of furniture or a support used to elevate the foot. Some footstools are designed for comfort, and others are designed for function. So, my enemies (footstool) are used to assist me to reach a place or area that I otherwise would not have been able to reach?

Wow! This has been a personal blessing and testimony for me. How can God make my enemies my footstool if I pray them away and they aren't within close reach? This requires obedience and a humble heart. I've experienced God using the same people who hurt me to be a blessing to me. The strong man is the one who wins any battle. If your flesh is stronger than your spirit, then your flesh will win the battles you fight.

This has certainly helped me in the area of spiritual maturity and forgiveness. A person's financial status, career, material possessions, or title won't prevent them from reaping what they sow. Galatians 6:7 says, "Do not be deceived, God is not mocked; for whatever a man sows, this he will also reap (NASB)." This holds true in the area of forgiveness as well. Forgiveness operates just like a bank account. Don't think about drawing from it if you haven't put any in.

God is our heavenly Father, so just think about it like this: no parent is pleased to see their children fighting or at odds with each other. But when a child demonstrates the things that their parent has taught them, it brings joy to the parent. God is love, and He is pleased with His children when we show forth love. The devil can't be forgiven or restored, so he uses the spirit of offense to keep the children of God from doing the things that are pleasing to God our Father. There is a process to forgiveness. I've experienced my so-called haters, enemies, and naysayers become a blessing to me. I knew this only happened because God's Word is true. God's love is perfected in you each time you choose to forgive.

Reflection Questions

1. Who do you need to forgive? Why?

2. In Colossians 3:13, what does the Bible say about giving and receiving forgiveness?

3. Do you believe you can forgive but don't have to forget? What does Isaiah 43:25 say about this?

CHAPTER 5
Value in the Valley

I endured years of emotional, mental, and physical abuse in the relationship I had with Amil. Going to church seemed to be a step in the right direction. Amil agreed to join me at church. He joined the music ministry and played the guitar. Just as things always were, victory came in small measures, and happy moments were short-lived. The abuse went to a new level, and I knew I had to get out while I was still alive.

This relationship had history. We were friends first, and we did all kinds of fun stuff together. If the relationship had not been abusive, I would have married him. I was totally in love, but I was also blind. He was controlling, and he wasn't afraid of anything or anybody. I knew he would never let anything happen to me. What I didn't know was that he would be the one I needed protection from. I wore black eyes like an article of clothing. I don't recall any triggers for this abuse. Sometimes it just came out of nowhere. I could say something he didn't like, and he would hit me in the mouth. My lip would take a few days to heal. If he felt threatened by anything or anyone, we would argue about it, and then I would have a black eye for a week or so. Between trying to hold down a job and a little side hustling, he stayed busy. When he wasn't working and was home more, the abuse seemed to increase.

I feared for my life. One day, I left with the clothes I had on my back, and Porshia and I went to my best friend's house to be in a safe environment. That didn't last long because he claimed I was keeping him away from his baby. He just wanted to spend a little time with her. He promised he would change his behavior, but I soon found out that was a lie.

I hadn't planned on returning, but I was another casualty of his manipulation. I reluctantly returned to the apartment for a visit, which was a huge mistake. I never should have gone alone. Once I got there and got Porshia situated, he wouldn't let me leave. He began to accuse me of being out with other men and assured me he wasn't going to lose me, and if he couldn't have me, then nobody would. That day, he assaulted me on the living room floor right in front of my baby. I woke up in the hospital beaten beyond recognition. My vocal cords were ruptured from the assault, and my uvula was damaged. It eventually had to be surgically removed. There was a police officer assigned to my room at the hospital because Amil was missing and so was my baby, Porshia.

Later that night, the police officer on duty informed me that a 911 call was dispatched to the apartment that Amil and I previously shared together. Amil had been shot in the apartment and was also rushed to the hospital. It was confirmed that Amil shot himself. He was in the hospital for several months. After Amil was released from the hospital, he was on the run from the law. That didn't last long. He served time in jail for the assault and was released a couple of years later. This ended our relationship, and I was back to square one.

This assault had me so fearful that I searched for immediate protection. I began to surround myself with people I thought would protect me. Although I was being abused, my new church family gave me hope that I was headed in the right direction. I told myself to just keep going.

Each time I hit a low or hard place, I had to push a little harder to not fall back into the same mindset.

I Am Redeemed

Redeemed Christian Center felt like a family. In fact, my new pastor and first lady, Pastor Kenneth and Sylvia Anthony, were good childhood friends with both of my parents. They loved me as if I were one of their own. They both hold a special place in my heart because they taught me so much over the years.

Pastor Kenneth was laid back and easy going. He was quick to give me grace in areas that I fell short. He always encouraged me and told me I was much greater than what I could see. By observing his posture and demeanor with others, I learned how to take charge and be a leader. He always treated me with respect in any setting. He preached a word that brought forth so much confirmation in my life, so I was being spiritually fed. I was learning God on a deeper level.

My first lady was quite the opposite. She was a classy lady who had fashionable taste. She wasn't laid back at all. She was structured and organized. A no-nonsense kind of woman. She meant business and always held me accountable by pushing me beyond my self-proclaimed limitations to show me that no matter how good I thought I was doing, I should always strive to do better. She was a strong-willed woman who had no problem giving direction on any occasion. Unlike the pastor, she wasn't quick to give grace. Her methods were stern, but she was effective in all her efforts. She taught me the art of worship. This was new to me and felt a little uncomfortable at first because the church I was raised in was a traditional church. At my home church, we sang devotional songs, choir songs, and praise songs but not worship songs. My first lady taught me that worship was a deep, intimate expression to God through my vocal obedience.

I'd been singing at Deliverance Mission since the age of seven. Singing had always been a passion of mine until my throat surgery. I prayed and asked God to return my passion for singing. First Lady Anthony was a teacher by nature and took great pleasure in teaching me how to tap into the realm of worship. This made me want to sing again. I became diligent and faithful in my duties at church, and I learned how to submit to leadership. All my roller coaster rides of good and bad seemed to be on the upswing.

Who Do You Say That I Am?

A part of learning to love me was to learn the meaning of my name. I never knew what my name meant. It was interesting to discover how many different translations and interpretations there are of my name. The name Keshia means "Favorite" and is of African origin. What was also interesting is that Keshia has a Hebrew origin. Keziah was one of Job's daughters in the Bible.

I found the Urban Dictionary's profile of my name to be interesting as well: *"Keshia is a girl who is really nice and shy. She will keep secrets and live life amazing. She is made fun of. Keshia will take things to heart. Once you get to know her she will finally start coming out of her shell. She can be loud at times. She will try to help you out as much as she can. She hates being disliked. She is a very caring person. She hates the attention and tries to get away from it. She thinks she is ugly when she is not. She doesn't like not being wanted. Keshia has 1-5 friends and loves them dearly. But most of all she is Beautiful."* The Arabic meaning of Keshia is "Woman alive, well, prosperous." The Albanian translation of KishE means "church." All of these definitions and translations revealed some interesting interpretations of my name, but I was still left with finding out who God says I am since He is the one who created me.

Learning who I am was important at this stage because I've heard so many negative interpretations and perspectives from those around me, and I unknowingly became what they defined me as. I always felt like I was created for greatness, but I wasn't sure how I would ever find it. God was the only one I could trust to guide me to the answers I so desperately wanted to find. Reading the Bible helped me learn who God says I am.

Psalm 139:14 says that *"...I am fearfully and wonderfully made...."*

1 Peter 2:9 says, *"But ye are a chosen generation, a royal priesthood, an holy nation, a peculiar people; that ye should shew forth the praises of him who hath called you out of darkness into his marvellous light...."*

Psalm 8:3–4 says, *"When I consider thy heavens, the work of thy fingers, the moon and the stars, which thou hast ordained; What is man, that thou art mindful of him?"*

I must be somebody special if the angels in heaven inquire of God, asking why He loves mankind so much. God's love toward me makes me want to know more about who He is and who He says that I am. He is my source for everything: *"By his divine power, God has given us everything we need for living a godly life. We have received all of this by coming to know him, the one who called us to himself by means of his marvelous glory and excellence..."* (2 Peter 1:3, NLT).

Not knowing the true source of something can hinder you in the area of operation. It's difficult to use something if you don't know what its function is. Knowing who you are gives you authority to operate in your specific gifts and talents. Sharing your gifts and talents with others will produce a plentiful harvest. Your ability to tap into your creative influence gives you power to fulfill your purpose. Being able to walk in your God-given purpose allows you access to kingdom connections. Kingdom connections are so much greater than the connections we create for ourselves. God takes us to the right places, connects us to the right people, to fulfills the right assignments.

I Give You All of Me

At this particular time, I actually wasn't interested in an intimate relationship or dating anyone. I had encountered enough relationships to know I wasn't good at picking guys. I had pretty much given up on that idea. I intentionally made it difficult for men to get close to me. I didn't hate guys or anything like that. I just had been hurt too many times to think I would be successful at it.

I met Michael, my current husband and the UPS driver who worked my loop of the mall. I saw him daily. Michael tried to get my attention, but I just wasn't interested. Trusting guys wasn't on my agenda, but Michael was excited to be challenged by each rejection. I have to admit that all the attention was flattering, but at this point, I still didn't know who I was. I was broken and shattered. I realized that I wasn't able to love anyone else until I was able to love myself first. I was so wounded from my relationship with Amil that all I was looking for in anybody or anything was protection and stability. I told myself I would never love again. Being vulnerable was for fools, and I wasn't going to allow my heart to hurt like that again.

Michael gave me his phone number several times, but I never called. He was persistent and did not spare himself any chance to ask why I hadn't called him yet because he wanted to take me out. I was flattered, and I thought to myself, What's the worst thing that can happen? Just go out with him once so he will leave you alone. So, I agreed to take him up on the offer. Little did I know when I did finally call him that it would be the start to our journey together as husband and wife. We dated for only a few months, and then we got married. Nobody could believe we were getting married. Actually, we couldn't believe it either.

Most said it wouldn't work. Some said we were stupid for getting married after dating for only a few months. Some asked why he was going to marry the hoe who had all those kids and three baby daddies. There was so much dirt thrown on our union that I didn't think he would marry me. Although I was learning more about who I was in Christ, I was still depressed and just kept putting a mask over the pain. I coped by staying busy, drinking alcohol, and eventually nurturing a marijuana addiction years later.

It was important for me to have a church family, so I invited Michael to my church. He quickly declined. He said he was raised in a household that didn't go to church, and he just wasn't interested. He had never experienced having a real relationship with God.

First of all, this was strange to me. I thought every kid went to church for Mother's Day, Easter, and Christmas. My feelings were a little hurt because going to church was all I really had going good for me, and he wasn't willing to give it any thought. If he is against something he hasn't even tried, I didn't want to waste my time on this relationship.

I called Michael on the phone and told him I couldn't see him anymore. He asked why, and I told him how I felt. I wasn't trying to change him as a person, so I wasn't going to make a big deal about it. But going to church was important to me, and if he didn't want to be a part of something that was so important to me, then we didn't have any type of future together. I had no patience or tolerance for anything moving forward. We didn't speak for a couple weeks.

Then I got a call one day, and it was Michael on the phone to tell me he took his suit to the cleaners and would be my guest at church that Sunday. I was overjoyed, and this was a small victory for me. It wasn't long before Michael joined me at Redeemed Christian Center and became a member.

Be Careful What You Ask For

Michael was raised as an only child and nurtured a selfish mentality most of his life. Michael's dearly departed dad, Odis C. Kirksey, was generally quiet and reserved, and his mom, Alice Lee, is sweet and firm all in one. We affectionately call her "Fluffy." In fact, she was the one who gave me my first middle name since I never had one. She calls me Keshia Mae.

His parents were both from the south and lived a conservative lifestyle. Both of Michael's parents lived during segregation and experienced picking cotton. They came from large families and only dreamed of leaving the south to start a family of their own as far north as they could go. They moved to Michigan. After years of unsuccessfully trying to have a baby, they decided to adopt Michael. They didn't realize that their hands were full with raising such a sweet but troubled little boy. Michael learned of his adoption at an early age and had many struggles as a result.

Michael is bi-racial and has never fit into his environment from childhood through adulthood. Michael often describes himself being too light for the black kids and too dark for the white kids. Michael was bullied as a kid and struggled to develop healthy social connections. He has always felt left out and not wanted. His adoptive parents loved him for sure, but the knowledge of his adoption negatively impacted him. Michael became angry by the rejection and began building walls at an early age. At one point, he became reckless and started selling drugs and stealing cars.

The course of Michael's direction changed, and he enlisted with the United States Marine Corp in 1984. Michael came home from the marines with plans on returning but decided to stay since he had a baby on the way. His firstborn was a beautiful baby girl named Ciara Kirksey. His relationship with his daughter's mother wasn't healthy, so they separated. Michael also has a son, Mackinley Watson, whom he never developed a relationship with.

Michael often carries a cocky aura about himself, but it's just a camouflage so people won't see his brokenness. His true self is tender and sensitive. The rejection and acceptance were so deeply rooted in him that he assumed nobody liked or loved him. Over time, all of these similar generational curses became more and more evident. Michael and I had a history of unhealthy relationships with our children. Michael wasn't active in either one of his kid's lives for many different reasons and neither was I. He was broken, and I was too. Michael felt rejected, and so did I.

I've learned from being broken that I'm drawn to other broken people. Subconsciously, I believed if I could make a difference in another broken person, maybe I could create some good from a bad situation. When I first married Michael, I wasn't in love. I liked him a lot and was learning to love him. I was only looking for protection and stability, and Michael graciously offered them both. I made it crystal clear before we got married: I wasn't having any more kids. I hadn't done right by my oldest two kids, so I didn't want any more children to suffer from this dysfunctional life of mine. I had done enough damage.

One day, out of the blue, my dear old mother-in-law tells me to have a seat at her kitchen table. She asked me to sit while she hurried off to a back room and was gone for what seemed like forever. When she came back to the kitchen, her face was flushed, and her eyes were glossy. She was holding a plastic bag in her hand. Wrapped in the plastic were the clothes Michael had on the day she picked him up from the orphanage. She told me the story about her life and marriage to her husband—she affectionately called him "Honey"—and how they tried for many years to have children before adopting Michael. She always dreamed of having lots of kids to love and spoil. Since she didn't get her wish, then maybe she would have better luck with grandchildren, she thought. That idea was short-lived since Michael didn't have a healthy relationship with his children.

My mother-in-law took careful detail in describing her heart's desires. She so badly wanted grandchildren to give her love to. She wanted to do things like have sleepovers, bubble baths, bedtime stories, and "...cook the best breakfast this side of heaven..." for them. But she didn't have any she could share all that love with, so she begged and pleaded for me to reconsider my decision to not have any more kids.

She promised if I had a baby she would take care of it, and I wouldn't have anything to worry about. I can still remember the tears she and I both shed together that day at that table. I was crying because I knew at that moment I loved this lady, and I was in a position to give her something she always wanted. Just like me, Michael thought it would be easier to just have another kid than to fix the relationship with the two kids he already had. He would occasionally out of the blue ask, "So, you wanna have my baby?" I said, "No," every time. We would get so tickled and laugh. However, we weren't laughing for long, because soon after I had the talk with my mother in law, Michael and I found out we were pregnant.

Several days before our second wedding anniversary, Michael and I took a trip to Wheels Inn for the weekend. We both heard great things about this place but had never been there before. Wheels Inn is an indoor amusement park in Chatham, Canada. As soon as we got settled into our room, my water broke, and my baby was on the way. I wasn't due yet, so we were both in a panic. We were given a full refund, and we headed back to the United States.

We made it back home, but our baby girl wasn't born until a couple days later, the day before our anniversary. Alece Odessa Kirksey was proof that God answers prayer. My mother-in-law was overjoyed, and she did everything she had promised she'd do.

I thought this baby was the answer to my problems, but I was wrong. We were still a young married couple carrying a lot of baggage. Before I knew it, the storm of despair returned even more demanding this time. I was blind to Michael's brokenness and developed false expectations of him. He was hurting just like me. It took many years before God allowed me to see how broken he really was. It was heartbreaking. I couldn't fix him, and he couldn't fix me. We promised no matter how hard or bad our marriage got, we would stick it out since none of our kids were raised with both parents. We were two years into our marriage, and the excitement was wearing off. We were faced with all the baggage we both brought into the marriage. It was so massive that we both began self-medicating our pain. Michael self-medicated with food, and I started smoking marijuana. Marijuana became my happy fix. It didn't matter how bad things were. If I took a few puffs, nothing else mattered.

We both stayed busy and worked under pressure to keep the attention off of our real issues. We focused more on our kids to redirect our dysfunction. We kept them busy in all types of activities, and it worked for a while until Michael lost his job and slipped into a deep depression.

Dysfunction Meets Grace

Depression seemed to be a common theme in my life, and now, it was showing up in my marriage. People perceive depression as clear and precise across the board, and that's just not true. I've heard people in their self-proclaimed righteousness make hurtful comments about this illness. Things like "Depression is a choice" or "You need to pray more." I certainly had not chosen to be a victim of sexual or physical abuse. Who in their right mind would want that for themselves?

What people who have not suffered from depression fail to realize is that once depression grips you, you've already exhausted all other hope of anything else. It's hard to come out of the cave of depression. I consider depression as a surface issue with a much deeper root. Depression has an origin; it comes from somewhere. People have chosen to judge me based on surface things but never find out the source of my hurt, pain, and brokenness.

Michael and I had that in common for sure. Depression has worked like a clogged valve in our marriage. Michael wouldn't let me in totally, and I wouldn't let him in totally. We just couldn't get anything to flow. We found ourselves nurturing each other's self-medicating habits just to have some level of sanity in our home. I would offer him more food, and he would offer me more weed. He was a little more tolerable when I was high, and I was easier to live with when he was eating what he wanted. So, we offered each other the thing that would give temporary satisfaction. Be careful with temporary satisfactions; they leave you empty and always searching for something else to fill that void.

Because Michael lost his job, we started having financial issues. We were facing foreclosure, and we weren't having sex at all. I shut down mentally and admitted myself to the Havenwyck Mental Hospital for evaluation. During my admission at Havenwyck, I met a lady who became my guardian angel. She was strong in both personality and character and did not hold her tongue. Speaking her mind was her area of genius. She took one look at me and asked me why I was there. She didn't even wait for a response before she answered for me. She quickly reminded me as if I already knew that I had no business being there. She said, "This is not a place for a beautiful girl like you."

She immediately became my personal spokesperson. I didn't speak for a day or two after I was admitted, so the staff was becoming impatient with me not responding. She answered everything they asked me as if she were responsible for me. She made sure to compliment me and encourage me the entire time I was there. It felt like she was a protective angel sent there just to make sure I would be covered. This was a God experience. Group therapy was a daily requirement at Havenwyck. One day, my guardian angel shared her story in group therapy. What she shared that day brought tears to my eyes. It became the proof I needed that I really didn't belong there.

The topic of that day was how we can make better choices so we don't end up coming back to the facility. She revealed that her mother was a drug addict and forced her to prostitute her body until she was eleven years old. She had enough and told her mom no more. Her mom took a knife and stabbed her nine times and left her in a pool of blood. She went through years of drug addiction after that incident until she got therapy to heal through those traumatic experiences.

I sat there in that moment, and no matter how low I was when I entered that place, I still knew without a doubt that I was created for something greater. Most people crave the mountaintop, but great lessons are learned in the valley. Most people perceive mountain experiences as positive and valley experiences as negative. My idea of a mountain experience was a direct result of what I survived in the valley. I thought the mountain experience was the time for me to celebrate the lessons I learned and the tests that I passed. While I was in the valley, I experienced judgment and rejection from others who were experiencing their mountain season.

My vision was limited in my valley experiences. I couldn't see the high places where others frequently traveled. I learned what not to do in the valley, and I learned what kind of heart I had in those low places. I observed those around me in a position to pour into me, but they chose not to because of their opinion and judgments of me. If I were in a position to bless those same people, I would do it in a heartbeat.

One time, while in the valley, I recall asking a girlfriend to borrow 20 bucks until Friday. She was offended by me asking and replied, "I'm really sorry, but I can't do that. You got a man, and I'm single." I had all the issues my marriage was struggling through, but she didn't see it that way. That was hurtful. In the valley, I felt as if I had nothing to offer others. I was humbled, and I learned how not to judge others. Their situation might look fabulous from the outside, but you don't know what you'll find when you peel back the layers. Since it was done to me and it didn't feel good, I promised not to ever make someone feel bad for having a need. It's only by God's grace that any of us are where we are.

After I was discharged from Havenwyck Mental Hospital, God began to use me to bless others in ways I never imagined. One by one, people were drawn to me. Some came by the house, and others called my phone. They all said they were blessed by my words of wisdom and encouragement. Some of the people who came for encouragement were the same people who had talked about and judged me.

As depleted as I was, it still felt good to be responsible for helping someone have a better day. If I could put a smile on somebody's face, it made me feel better too. I learned that even in the valley, offering others a different perspective to bring a positive solution gave me joy. This is one of the ways that God has shown me His purpose for my life. The things and people who hurt me were usually either a lesson or a test. Either way, I had to figure it out if I planned on passing the test or learning the lessons. When I didn't learn the lesson or I didn't pass the test, I had to repeat it all over again each time. I had repeated so many cycles until I was eager to find out how to end them. In the valley, I was depressed and had no strength. In the valley, I was exhausted and misunderstood. In the valley, I learned to walk by faith and not by sight. The valley experience revealed I was so much stronger than I thought I was. What I was going through in the valley wasn't about me. It was about God getting the glory out of what He called me to be.

God is so amazing in all of His infinite power. He knows our story from the beginning to the end. God gives seed to the sower. That means He needs to be able to trust you to sow seeds. It's hard to sow into someone you hold offenses toward. In Psalm 51:10, King David prayed and asked God to *"Create in me a clean heart, O God; and renew a right spirit within me."*

I would like to encourage you to pray the same prayer David prayed. Many offenses will come during our journey in life, but through the Word of God, our hearts can be cleansed of any such offense.

I have experienced God's grace and favor in deficient areas of my life. This level of blessings was only released after I would forgive someone who had hurt me badly. To partake in the blessing, I had to release the offense and give it to God. God is true to His word, and He keeps doing great things for me. No storm can last forever no matter where you are in life or what you may face. It's a lesson or a test, so just hang on. Help is on the way.

Reflection Questions:

1. What has kept you from forgiving the person/people you need to forgive?

2. What borders or walls have you created that prevent you from giving or receiving forgiveness?

3. How have you misunderstood any storms in your life that could have been God setting you up to be blessed?

CHAPTER 6
Cripple Can't Keep You from God's Promises

"But Jesus beheld them, and said unto them, With men this is impossible; but with God all things are possible."
– Matthew 19:26

After leaving the mental hospital, I was encouraged by what I had experienced and was on a new journey to find a meaning for all of this mess my life had produced. God had confirmed that He was always there, and He will always send help in times of trouble.

I'm reminded of a story in the Bible that speaks of a man named Mephibosheth. He was the son of Jonathan and the grandson of King Saul. The Bible records that after the death of Saul and Jonathan, Mephibosheth's nurse took him and fled in panic. In her haste, the child was dropped while fleeing. After that, Mephibosheth was lame and unable to walk again.

Many years later, David became king and inquired about any descendants of King Saul. It was customary in those days to kill the previous king's line. Instead, David wanted to honor them in memory of his friend Jonathan and out of respect for Saul. Saul's servant Ziba told him that Jonathan's son Mephibosheth was living in Lo Debar, which means "land of nothing." King David summoned Mephibosheth. *"'Don't be afraid,' David said to him, 'for I will surely show you kindness for the sake of your father Jonathan. I will restore to you all the land that belonged to your grandfather Saul, and you will always eat at my table.'"* (2 Samuel 9:7, NIV).

This story really blessed me because it's a story of redemption and restoration, which is just what I needed. Mephibosheth was not responsible for the thing that crippled him, and it landed him in a place that seemingly had him stuck. But God, in His grace and mercy, allowed favor to hit Mephibosheth's life, and he still ended up partaking in the blessings attached to his bloodline.

I saw myself in this story. I felt like somebody dropped me at a young age, and it crippled me in so many areas of my life. I've been stuck and experiencing "Land of Nothing" seasons throughout my life.

When I was a little girl, my mom said I could be whatever I wanted to be in life. She would ask me to think carefully about my future. This was a big concept for a young girl. After much thought, I replied with an answer she obviously wasn't expecting. I looked at my mom and said, "When I grow up, I want to be a lady!" I remember my mom laughing so hard she had tears in her eyes. My mom said the look on my face was of excitement and wonder as if I had discovered America.

In my young mind, being a lady always looked glamorous to me. A lady was somebody special. A lady was somebody who had power and was in control of her life. A lady was well-kept, beautiful on the inside and outside. I never talked about it much, but it was always my number one mission. And I wasn't going to stop until I became just that—a lady.

Finding Your Lady

Growing up, a neighbor across the street took a liking to me. Her name was Ms. Glenda. She was such a nice lady, and she seemed to have everything in the world. I looked up to her because I didn't know who I was, so looking at her made me want to be just like her when I grew up. Her house was super clean, so I couldn't figure out why she came to my house and asked my mom if I could come over for a few hours on the weekend to help her with household chores. She would pay me a few dollars. What I found out later was that God put her in my life to give me an example of what a balanced and organized lady looked like.

God takes care of His own. God gave me favor with Ms. Glenda, and she became a surrogate mother to me. She paid me so well that I thought it was robbery. I didn't really do much for the money, but it was God's way to pour into me through the words she would speak to me during those short few hours. She told me the most wonderful and positive things about myself that it seemed like she was talking about someone else. It felt good to hear it being said to me, so I eagerly awaited her affirmation and looked forward to my next encounter with her.

I continued to work for her until I got pregnant with my first baby. I felt like a huge disappointment because the things she poured into me were rich in nature, and she deserved to see the results of all her labor of love toward me. I had lots of work to do, but I was determined to be a lady some day. Many years later, I came into a greater understanding that being a lady wasn't just about being appealing to the eye. Being a lady is knowing you are enough. It's about discovering who you were created to be. A lady isn't intimidated by what she sees in others.

To find my lady, I had to be willing to try new things so I could discover what I did and didn't like. Being a lady meant fighting through negativity and letting my light shine. I've learned that finding out who you are will help you to discover your inner power. When you don't know who you are, you begin to mimic those whom you admire. It's much easier to copy others than it is to admit your inability to learn the basic attributes of who you are.

Knowing who you are is powerful and important. It helps you to navigate through life without the complications and voids that are attached to not knowing who you are. The core of your success depends on it. Knowledge of self strengthens your ability to avoid being manipulated by others. Your value is attached to who you are. Learning who you are is only the first step to understanding your value. I've often heard people say, "Just be you." What if you don't know who you are? You can't be someone you don't know.

Earlier, I talked about finding who you are in Christ, but what I didn't mention is that I had to commit to having an open perspective. This gave me room for trial and error. If I came across something I didn't like, I used it as an opportunity to learn. The open perspective allowed me to try new things without being afraid. I went to the movies alone. I went roller-skating alone. I went window-shopping alone. All of this alone time helped me to learn what I liked without any of the negative outside voices. Whatever little nickels I spent on the item I didn't like, I just told myself, "I'm building something, so these are small investment fees." It didn't take long before I knew all kinds of new things about who I was and what I liked.

Every time I got a paycheck, I went nail polish shopping. I wanted to know the simple things that made me Keshia. I tried all kinds of colors, and I was learning what colors I did and didn't like. I learned my favorite color is blue. Green is my least favorite color. I discovered that I'm not a pink kind of girl. I learned that the stylish clothes that look good on others often look funny on me. I've also learned that I'm a leader and I don't share the popular opinion of others. I took small steps and tried lots of different things over time and used this as an opportunity to learn something new about this Keshia girl.

After I ran out of colors and got bored with nail polish, I switched and started trying a different pair of cheap beauty supply store earrings. This continued until I started learning more and more about my likes and dislikes. It took patience, self-love, and forgiveness to find out who I really was. I began to identify my position in life and how I could add value to the world. My role didn't require me to control everything, but it was to be a good steward over what God had blessed me with.

The Bible has many examples of women God used in a mighty way, and I wanted to be one too. One of the greatest examples in the Bible is Mary the mother of Jesus Christ. God used her in a mighty way. Deborah was a prophetess and the only female judge mentioned in the Bible. Esther had courage and became a queen. Hannah had faith and made a covenant with God, and as a result, she birthed Samuel. Miriam was a prophetess. Ruth had unwavering faith, and God provided for her all the days of her life. Rachel was patient and was rewarded with the love of her life and children at an old age. These are just a few women God used. These women were not perfect. These women did not allow their situation or circumstances to dictate what they were willing to believe God for. That is how God gets the glory from our lives. I desire to also be used by God in a mighty way. Since God used these women in a mighty way, I believe He can use you and me like that too.

Reflection Questions:

1. In times you felt stuck or lost, can you remember what God used or sent to you during those times?

2. What things have you done to learn more about who you are as a person?

3. How do you respond to wanting to be used by God but not by man?

CHAPTER 7
Roots Run Deep

Frederick Douglass said, "It is easier to build strong children than to repair broken men." What a powerful statement that is. I believe everything starts at home. The first foundations we receive as children come from home.

Trust is an essential foundation in any relationship. When my trust was broken at such an early age, it intensified my level of distrust not only with people but also with places and things. Trusting affects so many things we say and do. Because I hadn't dealt with these issues, my trust issues became massive over the years and began to bleed from me like a gunshot wound. Finding purpose became my new mission.

I quickly learned a theory called "The Law of Attraction." A lady named Helena Blavatsky, who was a Russian Occultist, wrote a book in 1877, and this was the first record of this statement being used.

This became an important reason to heal from all my past hurt. Relationship after relationship, I continued to attract abusive guys. My body had healed, but my mind and emotions had not healed yet. Being wounded affects how you choose a partner. How I treated me taught others how to treat me. I've never heard of anybody introducing themselves and saying, "Hey, I'm abusive. Nice to meet you." Now, I know that sounds comical, but seriously, although it's never said, there is something unspoken that says it for you and puts that energy in the atmosphere. This is how the law of attraction works. It's not something that's said, but it speaks a language of its own. What we consciously or subconsciously submit ourselves to we ultimately become drawn to. The Bible confirms this in James 4:8: "Draw nigh to God, and he will draw nigh to you. Cleanse your hands, ye sinners; and purify your hearts, ye double minded."

I didn't know my own value, but I wanted others to know it. How crazy is that? Being wounded made me continue to look at what was on the outside instead of what was on the inside. Giving love didn't always guarantee I would receive it in return because I was expecting love from people who weren't taught how to love. I was also expecting love from people who were battling their own demons. I found out that having healthy and balanced relationships are only possible after you heal.

Healing is painful, but it is so necessary and essential. In order to move forward and be effective, internal healing must take place. The physical abuse heals faster than the other areas of abuse. The mental, emotional, and spiritual wounds stick around long after the physical scars disappear. Healing took strength and patience for me.

I found resources tailored to fit my specific needs, and they were beneficial during the healing process. For my spiritual needs, I went to church. This helped to build me up as a person through fellowship and support. For my mental needs, I saw a therapist, even though I was called crazy for seeking counseling. I've seen many therapists over the years. Choosing the correct therapist is important for progress so you don't cause yourself more pain by rehearsing traumatic events to the wrong person. I always prayed when seeking a therapist, and God always ordered my steps to just the right one.

Therapy should be tailor-made to the patient. Some people have more damage to work through, while others heal at a different pace. Therapy is like grieving in a sense. Nobody can really tell you how long it will take. You will know it when you get there. You will know it by what you still respond to in a negative way.

I recall a visit to one of my therapist's years ago. Although I don't remember her name, I will never forget her illustration concerning my mental healing. She used the analogy of a trash compactor. She explained to me the outcome of allowing trash to be compacted into my life without ever removing it. Can you imagine the terrible odor that is released?

The other thing she explained was that after a while, there was nowhere else for my trash to go, so it spilled out onto the floors of my life. Allow your imagination to visualize this. This hit close to home for me because I had all sorts of trash in my life that smelled awful, and I just didn't know how to empty all that. Besides, my trash was too heavy to lift, so I continued to live amongst stinky, filthy trash. At some point, the trash has to go out, or the mess and smell will contaminate every environment I occupy.

This was so true, and it caused my perspective to change. It gave me a visual to help me exercise the removal process of all of this trash I had collected all my life. As I was completing this chapter, the Holy Spirit allowed me to see the word therapist in a way I had never seen it before.

THERAPIST = The/Rapist

The interpretation that I received was mind-blowing. The Rapist strips you of your innocence, self-esteem, and confidence. Inversely, the job of the therapist is to help you strip away everything that has a negative impact on those same areas. Therapy isn't a replacement for God. Therapy is simply a resource to help build and repair broken areas and gives you a different perspective to why terrible things happen and how to reach a healthy mindset after experiencing trauma.

Emotions. Healing. Music.

Emotional healing has always been tough for me. Maybe this was the area I had suffered the most trauma. Getting better took more work. This was the only area that nobody could help me with except me. The emotional healing required building myself up. This wasn't so easy when I was in environments that tore me down. But I learned that the more you do anything, the better you can become, so I had to commit to doing the work.

Emotions are driven by our beliefs. I had to get myself to believe something different. This is where my creativity and imagination were activated. I envisioned myself rehearsing for a stage play. I developed an image in my mind of the person I wanted to be, and I would often practice how I dressed and how I spoke to and treated others. I traveled to other nearby cities where nobody knew me so that I could practice without the pressure of judgment. I practiced my methods at gas stations, grocery stores, beauty supply stores, restaurants, and many other places. I practiced being pleasant, graciously giving compliments, and trying hard to bring a smile to someone's face. It proved to create a positive response each time.

These passages remind me that this is God's battle, not mine. If I follow these steps on how to handle all of the people who hurt me, God will do the rest. He can do whatever He wants to do, but in most cases, my obedience is a prerequisite to His demonstration. I must first do my part.

This usually doesn't make sense to the carnal mind. To follow these instructions and understand what God is saying here means you understand these are spiritual weapons. This is the way the Word of God tells me to fight against the enemy and stay on the path to healing. When I don't put on the whole armor of God, I leave myself open for the enemy to defeat me. It's like a police officer not wearing a bulletproof vest in the line of duty. It could cost you your life when you're not protected. The devil doesn't play fair, so we must be equipped and safeguarded at all times.

The carnal man is constantly looking for ways to please self, while the spirit looks for ways to please God.

Whoever is the strongest will win. Whatever you feed is what will grow. As long as I focused on satisfying my flesh, then my flesh shaped my decisions. It wasn't until after being intentional about finding out what God's Word says about me that I was able to build my spiritual mindset and make decisions based on God's perception of me and not my own.

Flip the Script

My journey hasn't been easy by any means, but it's rewards are predicated on keeping a positive perspective and learning to do things God's way. For example, I continue to create new ways to grow my inner self. Over the years, Michael and I have worked hard on turning some of our negatives into positives. With all of the negative stigma attached to me having so many "Baby Daddies"—I have four—we made a joke to say he was the best baby daddy. We had so much fun with this one, and Baby Daddy became Michael's pet name.

I was convinced that because I was so broken, I was terrible at picking the right kind of guy for myself. So, I figured out what I would do. I was going to do a complete 360 and do the exact opposite. I was attracted to guys who had a dark complexion and had a little thug streak. I had never been with a light skin guy ever. Michael is not dark-skinned and neither was he thug. So, this was my plan I thought, but God had His own plan.

Michael was born at St. Joseph's Hospital of Mount Clemens, Macomb County, Michigan at 11:40 pm. At the time of his birth, his birth mother, who was a twenty-three-year-old Caucasian, and her husband thought it was in the best interest to put him up for adoption since her husband was not Michael's biological father. At the time of Michael's birth, his biological mother had two daughters ages three and five. Child and family services also documented that Michael's birth father was thirty-five years of age at the time of his birth and was of African American descent.

Michael was placed with four different foster care families during the adoption process and finally joined his adoptive family on June 20th, 1967.

In my opinion, Michael has always held a level of resentment toward women as a result of his perspective toward his birth mom. From Michael's perspective, I represent the mom who threw him away since I did the same thing to my baby. This attitude and perspective made things worse, and we couldn't figure out how to move forward after all of this trauma.

It wasn't long before the door was open, and I had an affair. The affair was short-lived because I became fearful Michael would soon find out, so I ended the affair and immediately exposed my infidelity to Michael. He became angry and displayed hatred toward me for a couple of years. He was coldhearted and denied me sex and all financial help or assistance. He stopped being nice to me, and every day seemed like hell.

I went back into depression and wasn't sure how we could fix it. I realized this was my fault because I was the one who had not been honest. We felt hopeless, so we allowed our flesh to take control. Soon, we were engaging in multiple sex partners and were introduced to swinging, the swapping of sexual partners within a group. When we first began, we started off together, and then we abandoned a few of the rules and began doing our own thing. Because we didn't have much of a physical attraction to each other, this seemed to be a temporary fix. The people we met in this lifestyle and the places we visited opened us up to all sorts of demonic activity.

At first, it seemed weird, but the people were friendly and accepting. My mind was blown to learn these were just regular ordinary people. The furniture store clerk, a bartender, a nurse, an engineer, and a Sunday school teacher were among a few of the people we had these sexual experiences with. Even in my sin, God was speaking to me.

He began to show me how to identify demonic spirits, what they look like and how they operate. I could see the spiritual warfare in these environments. I knew what I was doing was wrong, but my flesh was the strong man.

I was tired of hurting, so I only did what felt good at the time. This was the spirit of rebellion. It comes from unforgiveness, and this is what opened the door for other spirits to join in. I went too far and stayed too long. I prayed and cried after each encounter at first. I felt like it was filthy in nature, but I was so empty and was willing to trade my body for any temporary feelings of love or acceptance. I became so entangled in this web that I felt like prey waiting to be devoured.

The Apostle Paul tells us in Romans 7:18, *"For I know that in me (that is, in my flesh,) dwelleth no good thing: for to will is present with me; but how to perform that which is good I find not."*

Sin creates more generational curses. Michael and I both had strongholds that kept us divided from each other and from God. Each area of our life was dysfunctional and needed deliverance. The thing about sin is that it is appealing to the flesh. Our flesh was the strong man, so it governed every decision we made. When the excitement of our sinful activity wore off, our dysfunction exposed how deeply rooted our sin was and how desperately we needed God. Eventually, our sin began to cause other problems and added more issues to what was already there.

It was important to start closing doors to anything that reminded us or connected us to that kind of lifestyle and sin. Deleting phone numbers and contact information was important to remove these unhealthy connections. We both repented to each other and to God. It was also important to expose anything or anyone who tried to divide us in any way. We asked God to help us to find purpose and meaning for all of our dysfunction. God sent different people along the way to minister healing to our marriage who had no idea what we were facing.

I was twisted in a web of sin. I was so far gone, and I needed God to deliver me before I died in my sin. I started reading material on demonic spirits and spiritual warfare. I learned so many things that opened my perspective to how powerful I was in the spirit. I hadn't been taught how to use what I had for God's glory, so I was letting the devil use it for his gain. I had given him my body and my mind, but I still had something left. I still have my seed. My seed is the core of who I am. I have lived my entire life not knowing the value and worth of my seed. My seed provides nourishment that comes from God to feed every starving area in my life. The nourishment of my seed isn't just for me, but God intended to bless and nourish others as well.

God spoke to me during these times, and although I was still walking in darkness, His light was with me everywhere I went. I remember asking God how I got here. God showed me that the devil had attempted to destroy my life in the area of sexual attack. God said, "I am going to hold your hand this time around and walk you through the devil's territory." This season was training for my reigning. God was developing my purpose through all of these dark and terrible things that I had been through.

I came in contact with demonic spirits, and God gave me the boldness to speak His word in these evil dark places. I made sure to tell every demonic spirit that I belonged to God and that He has always covered me even in my sin, condemnation, and shame. After coming into the knowledge that I had been robbed blind by the devil for years, it gave me a sense of retribution against the devil. When I show love to myself and others after an attack or offense, it robs the devil of the victory of spreading the spirit of offense.

Sin causes isolation. Staying in that place of isolation for too long is dangerous. However, isolation is a good time for God to speak to you. When we are distracted by the noise of life, it's hard to hear the gentle, quiet voice of God. Finding time to get quiet and hear from God has given me direction, knowledge, and wisdom. God told me where to go for help. God connected me to total strangers with resources. God revealed the beauty of my scars.

I was in the valley when God taught me the power of endurance, patience, and forgiveness. I've learned to hear and know the voice of God in the valley. During these times, I could hear God whisper, "Hang on. Help is on the way." I realize that God was always right there every time I felt alone. Knowing that someone is always there gives me a sense of comfort and confidence.

Reflection Questions:

1. Can you identify any area(s) in your life where God has turned your negative into a positive?

2. How has God used the things you don't understand to bring Him glory?

3. In what areas(s) in your life can you trace sin as your bondage?

CHAPTER 8
When Nothing Else Could Help

Nourishment is essential for growth. When I think of the word "nourishment," it makes me think of all the things that may not be good to you but are good for you. The nourishment that comes from fruit is derived from its seed. My seed needs to reflect the fruit in my life. When someone observes my life, they should see qualities and features that demonstrate the fruits of the spirit.

The fruit of the Holy Spirit is a biblical term that identifies the nine characteristics of a person or community living in harmony with the Holy Spirit. Galatians 5:22–23 (NIV) lists these characteristics: *"But the fruit of the Spirit is love, joy, peace, forbearance (patience/tolerance), kindness, goodness, faithfulness, gentleness and self-control. Against such things there is no law."*

I believe that the seed of love contains the most nourishment. In 1 Corinthians 13:13 (NIV), it says, *"And now these three remain: faith, hope and love. But the greatest of these is love."* Love is mentioned in the King James Version of the Holy Bible 310 times—131 times in the Old Testament and 179 times in the New Testament.

We know that power is produced from love because Jesus Christ died on the cross because of His love for all of His children. I am His child, so He paid that price just for me. The same applies to you. Every time we show love to others, we not only demonstrate the love that God placed inside of us but also honor the sacrifice of the blood of Jesus Chris that was shed for us.

John 13:35 tells us, *"By this shall all men know that ye are my disciples, if ye have love one to another." So, when I look past the faults, judgments, and pain caused by others and choose to show God's unconditional love, I allow God's light to shine through me. Jesus reminds us to "Let your light so shine before men, that they may see your good works, and glorify your Father which is in heaven"* (Matthew 5:16).

Finding out the differences between the fruit of the spirit and the fruit of the flesh is important when fighting against the enemy. When you learn that God is love, joy, and peace, then you won't allow someone to operate in hatred toward you and not identify it. When you understand that the devil has attributes of confusion, envy, strife, and jealousy, then you won't allow anyone to tell you it's God when these things are present.

Learning how to fight against the devil requires you to learn about spiritual weapons. For example, if someone did something hurtful against me, the God thing to do would be to forgive them, pray for them, and still treat them with love and kindness. On the other hand, if I allow my flesh to rule and operate out of the same spirit the devil operates in, then I have given in to his tactics, and I'm now obeying him instead of God. It requires me to be humble and not think more of myself than others. This is how I honor God and fight against the devil. Love is a powerful weapon, and the devil is no match for God's love.

I frequently look for ways to prove the devil wrong. For many years while I was suffering from depression, the devil used to try and make me believe nobody loved me. I went on a mission to prove him wrong, and every time someone bought me a greeting card, I would save it and toss it in a huge bag. Over the years, I have begun to look back and see for myself just how many people really do love me. How many people left their house and took time to pick out just the right card. Whether the card was mailed or hand-delivered, my point was proven: I am loved.

I looked at these as spiritual exercises. Continued practice would ensure that my love muscle was growing. God's love is so powerful that it can pull you out of any circumstance and condition. I am reminded of an old-time favorite hymn that I learned as a little girl:

"Love Lifted Me"

I was sinking deep in sin, far from the peaceful shore,
Very deeply stained within, sinking to rise no more;
But the Master of the sea heard my despairing cry,
From the water lifted me, now safe am I.
Love lifted me! Love lifted me!
When nothing else could help,
Love lifted me.
Love lifted me! Love lifted me.
When nothing else could help,
Love lifted me.

This popular sacred hymn, written by James Rowe in 1912, has ministered to me for many years. The lyrics to this song mirror my life. It's encouraging to know that no matter where I am in my life and what I've done, the Master lifts me out of any and all despair with His love. You can't tell me love isn't powerful. Because God is omniscient (all knowing), He knows what needs to be put inside of me and what needs to be removed in order for me to be the woman that He intended for me to be. God knew before I was born that I needed to walk in His love so that I could fulfill His purpose for my life. In order to walk in God's love, I had to be willing to abandon my warped belief system of what I thought love actually was.

Denying our fleshly desires in order to be more like Christ is a spiritually mature mindset that produces results. We can only do this by embracing His love.

Through years of depression, God's love has kept me. I felt deprived of love. so that's the area that I needed God to fill me in. I'm still in my right mind because of God's love for me. There was a specific purpose for my confusion, depression, and despair. It was all for his glory. God's love shines through me today, and I honor the sacrifice of His love toward me.

Reflection Questions:

1. Does your seed produce fruits of the spirit or fruits of the flesh? List how many you can identify in your own personal life.

2. Share any situation or circumstance that God's love had to lift you out of.

3. Think of and list how many ways you can deny your fleshly desires.

CONCLUSION

I've spent my entire life trying to figure out the why. Why am I different? Why did bad things happen to me so early in life? Why do I feel so rejected? Why have I always felt so empty inside? Why can't I move past having trust issues? Why am I always misunderstood? Why can't I receive the same love I give? Why haven't I been able to figure out my purpose? Because of God's specific plan for my life, He knew that every situation and circumstance I encountered was necessary for His plan for me. Nothing can happen without God's permission. Every broken area of my life was designed to be a weapon against the kingdom of darkness.

When God brings deliverance to any area of your life it's not for you to cast judgment. We are to share His goodness and show His love. My dear brothers and sisters, we are all created for a unique design and purpose. Although we may never understand the things we must encounter along our journeys and the methods God uses to get us to the place He wants us to be, we must have faith in His Word and what it declares over our lives. The devil has already been defeated, so his purpose is to deceive you into joining his losing team.

Every broken area of my life was broken on purpose by God before the foundations of the earth. All of my broken pieces represent a powerful weapon against the kingdom of darkness. This is why the devils assignment has been so great against my life. But as always, God is greater.

I thank my Lord and Savior Jesus Christ for all of His many blessings He has so graciously given to me. I don't deserve any of His goodness, but His grace and mercy have followed me throughout my life. For this, I am grateful. His quiet whisper has been a constant in my ear no matter how near or far I felt from Him. The struggle has been great because God's reward for my life is great.

I thank God for giving me strength to fight and overcome every plot and tactic of the devil. I've spent most of my life not understanding that my pain was attached to my purpose. The pain I've endured throughout my life has created a passion for others who hurt in the same area. Now that God's healing power is manifesting in my life, it's time to do what His grace saved me to do. I serve notice to the devil that every hurting or abused person whom God allows me to come in contact with is going to be loved and encouraged by God's love through me.

This is why I was broken for battle.

ACKNOWLEDGEMENTS & THANK YOU

I would first like to thank God for His love and kindness toward me. His grace, mercy, and favor have found themselves attracted to me throughout my life and served as proof that God uses broken things all of the time for his glory.

To each of my children—Chris, Shavonne, Porshia, Devon, and Alece—I love you. I acknowledge there are many areas where I fell short as a mom. I made lots of bad decisions, gave depression years that belonged to you, and stayed stuck too long. I'm sorry for all the hurt and neglect that I caused you along the journey of finding out who I am. Thanks for forgiving me and allowing God to restore the years that we have lost.

To my entire family, there are far too many of you for me to list you all individually, so collectively, I love and thank God for each of you. My family has watched me both from near and from afar. They have seen me up, and they have seen me down. I thank you all for your individual roles in my life. The love that we all share for each other is both real and rare no matter what tactics the devil has tried to use. I thank you all for choosing to love me through all of my storms. Your prayers were not in vain. They served as water in a dry place.

To Bishop Kenneth Anthony and Pastor Sylvia Anthony, I find it hard to express my gratitude, so I will simply say thank you. You both have poured years of valuable lessons and love into me. Your spiritual instruction and guidance through the spirit of love guided me through some dark and weary days, and for that, I am grateful.

A special thank you to my spiritual godmother, Evangelist Ormellia Reynolds. I thank you for your constant encouragement and endless prayers. Your love for God has allowed you to only see me through a spiritual lens. I love you.

To the best writing coach this side of heaven. Thank you, brother Jesse Cole Jr. of Kingdom Mogul Coaching. You were sent by God to take my hand and walk me through the process of writing. Your practical illustrations and encouragement along with accountability has given me a new perspective on the spirit of excellence through obedience. I thank you for all you've poured into me from start to finish.

I realize that I did not overcome every battle and every situation alone. It really does take a village. I'm grateful to God for the men and women along my journey who I've been privileged to be mentored by. I thank God for every person who influenced me in a positive way, and when I look back over my life, God always sent someone to love me, lift me, and encourage me. I'm grateful for every valley experience, every attack, and every season.

I also want to thank my "Baby Daddy," Michael Kirksey, for your commitment to stay in this fight with me. This journey hasn't been easy, so thanks for staying through every misunderstanding, every painful situation, and every mountain that we have encountered. There is a special level of anointing required to nurture and love a broken person. Thank you for loving me. There have been times that love didn't seem to be enough. When trials seem to have no end and hope was diminishing fast, God's hand was strategically taking our dysfunction and using it for His glory. Thank you for being a part of my Kingdom assignment and walking with me through these seasons of healing and harvest.

Last but certainly not least, I want to thank myself. I thank Keshia Mae for forgiving herself after all the unforgivable things she has done. I thank Keshia Mae for finally affording herself the privilege of getting to know and loving such a wonderful person. I thank Keshia Mae for having the courage to heal and see past all the pain she has experienced. I thank Keshia for just being Keshia.

I am grateful to be called.
I am grateful to be anointed.
I am grateful to be favored by God.
Because I was broken for battle!